Book One Of The "Heaven Now" Series

Present Access To Heaven

Propiv Press
Lancaster Pennsylvania, USA

Present Access To Heaven

By Jonathan Brenneman

Present Access To Heaven

Copyright © 2016 by Jonathan Brenneman. All rights reserved. This book is protected by the copyright laws of the United States of America. This book may not be copied or reprinted for commercial gain or profit. The use of short quotations or occasional page copying for personal or group study is permitted and encouraged. Permission will be granted upon request.

General Editor Arnolda M. Brenneman
Contributing Editor John Lee

Propiv Press, Lancaster, Pennsylvania, USA

ISBN-13: 978-1537643540
ISBN-10: 1537643541

Printed in the United States of America.

Unless otherwise indicated, scripture quotations are taken from the New Revised Standard Version Bible, copyright © 1989 the Division of Christian Education of the National Council of the Churches of Christ in the United States of America. Used by permission. All rights reserved.

Scripture quotations marked AMP are taken from the Amplified® Bible Copyright © 2015 by The Lockman Foundation. Used by permission. Scripture quotations marked ESV are taken from The Holy Bible, English Standard Version® (ESV®) copyright © 2001 by Crossway Bibles, a publishing ministry of Good News Publishers. Used by permission. All rights reserved. Scripture quotations marked GW are taken from GOD'S WORD®, © 1995 God's Word to the Nations. Used by permission of Baker Publishing Group. Scripture quotations marked KJV are taken from the 1769 King James Version of the Holy Bible, Public Domain. Scripture quotations marked NIV are taken from THE HOLY BIBLE, NEW INTERNATIONAL VERSION®, NIV® Copyright © 1973, 1978, 1984, 2011 by Biblica, Inc.® Used by permission. All rights reserved worldwide. Scripture quotations marked RSV are taken from the Revised Standard Version, copyright ©1962 by the World Publishing Company. All rights reserved. Scripture quotations marked YLT are taken from Young's Literal Translation of the Holy Bible by J. N. Young, 1862, 1898, Public Domain. Scripture quotations marked Phillips are taken from The New Testament in Modern English by J.B Phillips copyright © 1960, 1972 J. B. Phillips. Administered by The Archbishops' Council of the Church of England. Used by Permission. Scripture quotations marked NKJV are taken from the New King James Version®. Copyright © 1982 by Thomas Nelson. Used by permission. All rights reserved.Scripture quotations marked NASB are taken from the NEW AMERICAN STANDARD BIBLE®, Copyright © 1960, 1962, 1963, 1968, 1971, 1972, 1973, 1975, 1977, 1995 by The Lockman Foundation. Used by permission.

Excerpts from "The Hiding Place" are taken from "The Hiding Place" by Corrie Ten Boom, Elizabeth Sherrill, and John Sherrill. Copyright © 1971 and 1984 by Corrie Ten Boom and Elizabeth and John Sherrill. Copyright © 2006 by Elizabeth and John Sherrill. Published by Chosen Books, a division of Baker Publishing Group. Used by permission.

This book is not intended as a substitute for the medical advice of physicians. The reader should regularly consult a physician in matters relating to his/her health and particularly with respect to any symptoms that may require diagnosis or medical attention.

Dedication

I dedicate this work to Jesus our savior, who gave his body to be torn so that we could enter heaven itself.

Book One in the "Heaven Now" trilogy

Present Access To Heaven

Table of Contents

1. Present Access To Heaven 1
   - *The Power Of God Unto Salvation* *1*
   - *How I Was First Saved* *7*
   - *Ongoing Salvation In My Life* *11*
   - *Heaven Itself* *14*
2. God's Glory And Heaven 19
   - *Heaven Is Where God Is* *19*
   - *The Tree Of Life* *21*
   - *The Tree Of The Knowledge Of Good And Evil* *28*
3. Growing In The Knowledge Of The Lord 35
   - *Present Heavenly Realities Accessible Through The Gospel* *35*
   - *Continuing In Our Salvation* *39*
   - *The Passion Play* *42*
   - *The Full Measure Of The Stature Of Christ* *46*
4. Removing The Veils 49
   - *What Are Veils?* *49*
   - *The Old Covenant Law* *52*
   - *Sin, Guilt, And Shame* *55*
   - *Unforgiveness* *61*
   - *Emotional Numbness* *66*

Lies Which Exalt Themselves Against The Knowledge Of God 70

5. The Vision **73**

Why Do I Feel Frustrated? 73

Toronto 74

Banging On The Wall Of Heaven 74

The Interpretation 75

Oh, That You Would Rend the Heavens and Come Down! 77

Trying To Bring Christ Down From Heaven Or To Bring Him Up From The Dead 79

Ascending Into Heaven Or Descending Into The Abyss. 80

The Dangers Of Descending Into The Abyss 83

The Word Is Near You.. 87

The Fruit Of This Teaching.. 88

6. Dead To The Earthly Man, Resurrected As A Man Of Heaven... **91**

The First Adam And The Second Adam 91

No Longer Mere Men... 97

Put Off The Earthly Man And Put On The Man Of Heaven 99

7. Heavenly Realities **103**

The Fullness Of God 103

The Hope Of His Calling 104

Releasing Hope 115

The Riches Of The Glory Of His Inheritance In The Saints 116

Our Inheritance.. 119

Understanding The Glorious Riches Of Our Present Inheritance *124*

The Immeasurable Greatness Of His Power To Us Who Believe *128*

8. Righteousness, Peace And Dominion **137**

More Heavenly Realities *137*

Peace And Salvation *138*

Righteousness And Peace *139*

Peace And Your Dominion As A Man Of Heaven *140*

Peace-Heaven's Reality *145*

Dominating Your Environment With The Peace Of God *147*

9. Heavenly Minded **151**

Set Your Minds On Things Above *151*

Rejecting Self-Pity *157*

Making The Maimed Whole *160*

Conclusion *165*

About The Author **169**

Contact **171**

Also By Jonathan Brenneman **172**

1. Present Access To Heaven

The Power Of God Unto Salvation

Romans 1:16 (NIV) For I am not ashamed of the gospel, because it is the power of God that brings salvation to everyone who believes…

The word *"salvation"* in scripture is rich with meaning. In the New Testament two Greek words are commonly translated as *"salvation"*—*soteria* and *sozo*. A scriptural word study of every use of both these words in the New Testament shows they are very practical words! The meaning of *sozo*, in particular, is multifaceted. Following are two of the most well-known scriptures which translate *sozo* as *"saved"*:

Romans 10:9-10 (NIV) If you declare with your mouth, "Jesus is Lord," and believe in your heart that God raised him from the dead, you will be saved. For it is with your heart that you believe and are justified, and it is with your mouth that you profess your faith and are <u>saved</u>.

Ephesians 2:8-9 (NIV) For it is by grace you have been <u>saved</u>, through faith—and this is not from yourselves, it is the gift of God—not by works, so that no one can boast.

This same word, *sozo*, is also often translated *"made whole"* or *"healed."* It's used several times in the gospels and in Acts in the context of physical healing.

It's also used to describe deliverance from demons. In one place it is even used in the context of raising the dead. It's not merely a spiritual word, but is tangible in its practicality. Here are a few examples. In the following verses, the underlined words are translated from the word *sozo*.

Mark 6:56 (NIV) And wherever he went—into villages, towns or countryside—they placed the sick in the marketplaces. They begged him to let them touch even the edge of his cloak, and all who touched it were <u>healed</u>.

Luke 8:36 (NIV) When they came to Jesus, they found the man from whom the demons had gone out, sitting at Jesus' feet, dressed and in his right mind; and they were afraid. Those who had seen it told the people how the demon-possessed man had been <u>cured</u>.

Luke 8:49-50 (NIV) While Jesus was still speaking, someone came from the house of Jairus, the synagogue leader. "Your daughter is dead," he said. "Don't bother the teacher anymore." Hearing this, Jesus said to Jairus, "Don't be afraid; just believe, and she will be <u>healed</u>."

Acts 27:30-31 (NIV) In an attempt to escape from the ship, the sailors let the lifeboat down into the sea, pretending they were going to lower some anchors from the bow. Then Paul said to the centurion and the soldiers, "Unless these men stay with the ship, you cannot be <u>saved</u>."

Salvation includes much more than having your name written in the book of life so you go to heaven when you die. That's only one aspect of salvation! The salvation that God offers includes deliverance, peace, wholeness, healing, and all that is in heaven. It touches every part of our being.

I also examined every scriptural use of the Hebrew word for peace, *shalom*. The contexts are clear that *shalom* is also a practical word. It's used in speaking of provision, health, and well-being in every way. The Greek word *sozo* and the Hebrew *shalom* are very similar in meaning.

Scripture teaches that we have been saved, that we are being saved, and that we are awaiting salvation. Therefore, salvation is something that has been accomplished, it is a process that's happening, and it's a hope that we are awaiting. For example:

Past
Ephesians 2:8 (NIV) For it is by grace you have been saved...

Titus 3:5-7 (NIV) He saved us, not because of righteous things we had done, but because of his mercy. He saved us through the washing of rebirth and renewal by the Holy Spirit, whom he poured out on us generously through Jesus Christ our Savior, so that, having been justified by his grace, we might become heirs having the hope of eternal life.

Present
1 Corinthians 1:18 (NIV) For the message of the cross is foolishness to those who are perishing, but to us who are being saved it is the power of God.

2 Corinthians 2:15 (NIV) For we are to God the pleasing aroma of Christ among those who are being saved and those who are perishing.

1 Peter 1:8-9 (NIV) Though you have not seen him, you love him; and even though you do not see him now, you believe in him and are filled with an inexpressible and glorious joy, for you are receiving the end result of your faith, the salvation of your souls.

Future

Romans 5:9-10 (NIV) Since we have now been justified by his blood, how much more shall we be saved from God's wrath through him! For if, while we were God's enemies, we were reconciled to him through the death of his Son, how much more, having been reconciled, shall we be saved through his life!

Romans 13:11 (NIV) And do this, understanding the present time: The hour has already come for you to wake up from your slumber, because our salvation is nearer now than when we first believed.

1 Peter 1:5 (NIV) ...who through faith are shielded by God's power until the coming of the salvation that is ready to be revealed in the last time.

In this book I emphasize the present aspect of salvation; that we are being saved. Evangelicals often emphasize that we were saved, which is true. We were washed with Christ's blood, justified, and born again when we first turned to Christ.

However, as we continue to look to Christ his redemptive work continues to transform us and renew our souls, bearing the fruit of righteousness, peace, and joy in our lives. There is both a finished work, and a continual outworking of the grace of God in our lives.

Hebrews 10:14 (NIV) For by one sacrifice he has made perfect forever those who are being made holy.

Chapter One—Present Access To Heaven

I remember when the Gospel message first became real to me. I understood God's love; that while I was still a sinner, Christ died for me.[1] When Jesus gave me a new heart it felt like heaven opened over me. Peace and joy flooded my soul! The things I had hated about myself and tried so hard to change were gone.

In the twenty years since then, I have never gotten tired of hearing the gospel! It continues to strengthen and empower me to do what I can't do on my own. After heaven first opened to me I stumbled, and spent far too much time not living in peace but in torment.

God and his faithfulness never changed! But I stopped looking to Him, and so I needed to hear and believe the gospel again, and to hold fast to its truth. As we continue to believe and embrace gospel truth, it continues to bear fruit in our lives and bring us peace and life.

Colossians 2:6 (NIV) So then, just as you received Christ Jesus as Lord, continue to live your lives in him...

Hebrews 4:16 (NIV) Let us then approach God's throne of grace with confidence, so that we may receive mercy and find grace to help us in our time of need.

Christ, by his sacrifice, has given righteousness to all who put their faith in him, allowing us full access to the Father's presence. If we continue to live our lives in Christ just as when we first received him, we will continue to freely approach God's throne of grace with confidence. As we regularly draw near to God, through

---

[1] Romans 5:8

Christ, heavenly rivers of mercy, grace, and love will flow into our beings and, through us, to the world.

John 7:38 (NIV) Whoever believes in me, as Scripture has said, rivers of living water will flow from within them.

God has given us immeasurable wealth in Christ. Attempting to comprehend such vast treasure is mindboggling. However, when we fail to live our lives in harmony with gospel truth we experience much less than what is possible! In doing so we lose sight of the fullness that God has given us. We no longer believe God's potential through us because we get so used to living far below it!
    My aim in writing is that we would have a renewed understanding of the gospel and the present possibilities it brings us as we continually approach God the Father through Christ. What is possible for us right now is exceedingly glorious. It's difficult to imagine because it's so far greater than anything we have yet lived.
    Indeed, these truths continue to challenge me. I have lived them to some degree, but I need to do so all the more! Let's take hold of everything that God has given us in Christ!

1 Timothy 1:6 (NIV) Fight the good fight of the faith. Take hold of the eternal life to which you were called when you made your good confession in the presence of many witnesses.

1 Corinthians 15:1-2 (ESV) Now I would remind you, brothers, of the gospel I preached to you, which you received, in which you stand and by which you are being

Chapter One—Present Access To Heaven

saved, if you hold fast to the word I preached to you—unless you believed in vain.

How I Was First Saved

I grew up in a Christian family. My mother taught all of us kids to memorize scriptures, and also sang praise and worship songs with us at night. We memorized something called the *"Roman's Road"* to salvation.

Romans 3:23 (NIV) For all have sinned and fall short of the glory of God.

Romans 6:23 (NIV) For the wages of sin is death, but the gift of God is eternal life in Christ Jesus our Lord.

Romans 5:8 (NIV) But God demonstrates his own love for us in this: While we were still sinners, Christ died for us.

Romans 10:9-10, 13 (NIV) If you declare with your mouth, "Jesus is Lord," and believe in your heart that God raised him from the dead, you will be saved. For it is with your heart that you believe and are justified, and it is with your mouth that you profess your faith and are saved...for, "Everyone who calls on the name of the Lord will be saved."

I heard this message multiple times as a child, and prayed several times to *"ask Jesus into my heart."* Yet I never felt peace. I was often angry and had fits of rage. I was selfish, and developed a shoplifting habit. I felt guilty about all this. Even though I prayed for God to forgive me, I felt like I could not change what I did.

I first read the Bible when I was seven years old. Although I enjoyed portions of it, other parts intensified my feelings of fear and guilt.

I wasn't sure if God really existed, but I was afraid that I would go to hell if he did. I remember sitting on the grass in a field as a kid and wondering if God was real and created the world or if it was formed by evolution. I concluded that evolution was impossible, but if God created the world, where did God come from? So neither one made sense to me.

One morning when I was eight or nine years old, I woke up with pain in my back. I'm not sure what caused it, but it was much worse than a temporary pain caused by sleeping the wrong way. I went downstairs because my mom was going to give me a haircut.

When I sat down, I said *"Mom, my back is killing me!"* She responded *"Why don't I pray for it?"*

I was a little surprised, and said *"OK,"* but I was thinking *"Whatever. I guess you can try if you think it will do something."* I didn't expect anything more than a little religious ritual. She put her hand on my back and said *"In Jesus' name, pain leave now."* When she said that, I felt a ball of energy rolling up and down my spine, inside my back.

Bewildered, I asked *"Mom, what are you doing?"* She answered *"I'm not doing anything. God is healing you."* When she momentarily left the room, I still felt the thing rolling up and down. It slowed down and faded away, and the pain was gone. Then I realized that my mom didn't do anything, but God healed me. That was how I became convinced of God's existence.

For some time I was even more afraid of going to hell. I now knew God was real, but I felt like I couldn't change myself or stop shoplifting. Then, when I was ten years old, I went to a Christian camp for children and teenagers called Circle K.

My grandmother paid my way. I really didn't want to go, but my parents made me. However, it was a wonderful place when I went! The people who ran that

Chapter One—Present Access To Heaven

camp were the most fun people I had ever met, and they were overflowing with God's love! It seemed that their faces were glowing with love and kindness. I remember how much it meant to me that one of the ladies who led the camp, Vicky, remembered my name. I didn't think she would so readily know my name among so many other kids.

The day and night were full of fun activities, rough games, swimming, capture the flag, big shaving cream fights, and more. I also found out that I was really good at foosball![2] There were morning and evening chapel meetings. We sang praise and worship songs and Vicky's husband, Bob, preached to us. After every morning chapel meeting, we all went to sit at a spot in the woods for 15 minutes to read our Bibles.

I loved this place. I loved sitting in the woods reading my Bible and going to chapel. I felt a level of peace I had never experienced. The joy that these people had was contagious.

At night, Bob preached about how Jesus suffered and died a horrible death to deal with our sin so that we could have peace with God. I remember children weeping, deciding to give their lives to Christ. I felt the glory of God and it was like heaven to me. The message of the gospel touched my heart in a way it never had before, and I decided that I wanted to give my life to Jesus.

My cabin counselor was a friendly guy named Mike. He was soon to leave as a missionary to Papua New Guinea to teach the gospel to stone-age tribespeople. Mike gave me a quarter to buy an ice pop and told me that in the same way, God's gift of salvation was free. All I had to do was receive it. I decided that I wanted to become a missionary too.

---

[2] Known by Brits as "table football."

However, when I got back home after that week, it seemed that everything was even worse. I felt like I couldn't stop stealing, and I had no peace.

The next year, I returned to the same camp. I don't remember any time I prayed, or any super-spiritual experience. I just had lots of fun. I played foosball and capture the flag, and I enjoyed singing songs in chapel and the devotional time in the woods. I felt God's love and God's goodness there.

When my parents came to pick me up, I was really down because I liked being at camp and didn't want to leave. Halfway home, we stopped to go hiking on the Appalachian Trail. When we got out of the car, my mom saw how depressed I was and said *"Jonathan, what is there to be sad about?"*

When she said that, I thought back to myself, *"Yeah, what is there to be depressed about?"* I didn't pray a prayer, but when that happened, it felt like heaven opened over me and joy and peace descended on me.

I guess that maybe it was just the moment when in my heart I was tired of living my selfish life and I preferred to live Christ's life, which I saw demonstrated when I was at that camp. When I went home, I was a different person. I never struggled to stop shoplifting again; it was gone. I believe this was when I was *"born again."*

The first thing I remember doing when I got home was washing the dishes and sweeping the floor. Nobody asked me to. Before that I would complain when my mom wanted me to do chores, but now I wanted to help. Ever since then I have liked washing the dishes! I also began sleeping with my Bible under my pillow so I would remember to read it the next day.

Chapter One—Present Access To Heaven

Ongoing Salvation In My Life

It was about a year until I fell back into fear and condemnation. I was hitting puberty and began to struggle with lust. I became terrified that I had committed the unforgiveable sin by rejecting God's grace in my life, and could not be saved!

Again the Lord delivered me, showing me his love and grace. I was about 13. Some people who had been at Toronto Airport Christian Fellowship in Canada were guest speakers at our church. I again felt God's goodness, and this time I felt God's love envelop me so that my hands and face were literally vibrating with it.

God showed me that he not only loved me and forgave me, but that I would do many miracles in Jesus' name. I dreamed of taking the hands of a cripple, like Peter did in the book of Acts, and saying *"What I do have I give you. In the name of Jesus Christ of Nazareth, walk."*[3] This dream would later be fulfilled.

Soon after this I went on a trip to Mexico and fell in love with the people. I became zealous about becoming a missionary, and I started to learn Spanish. I also began reading 21 chapters of the Bible a day.

However, I fell into extreme legalism and still was not free from feelings of shame and guilt. If I had been a religious leader, I would have been leading a cult! The inner turmoil I felt led me to the point of desperation. Then the Lord dealt forcefully with my legalism.

When I was 15, I again experienced God's presence as a powerful love, so strong I could physically feel it. The Lord delivered me from guilt and condemnation, and from the bondage of legalism. Looking back, I realize I was also set free from Obsessive-Compulsive Disorder.

---

[3] Acts 3:6

In the following months I felt such love in my heart that I wondered *"How is it possible for me to love so much?"* This profoundly affected how I related to people. I saw the fruits of the Spirit like love, joy, peace, and gentleness manifest in my life.

I continued to go on mission trips to several countries and to study languages. When I was 17, I took my first of several trips to Belize. Before my second trip to Belize, I was in much prayer for the salvation of that nation and I felt a great burden of heaviness and anguish.

Then the Lord taught me from scripture about praise and thanksgiving. When I put those truths into practice, they again led me into what I would call *"heavenly experiences."* These were not visions or out of body phenomena. Rather, I experienced God's love and goodness so that I felt a joy and ecstasy no words could describe.

Experiencing God's glory was like swimming in water. I often felt it physically, as a weight that was resting on me, as a current flowing through me, or as a vibration in the surrounding atmosphere that I felt on my face and hands.

I had some trials and disappointments over the next few years. By the time I was 20, I felt desperately dry. I was disillusioned with the church, and frustrated with myself. Even though I'd often prayed and even fasted, I had never laid hands on anybody and seen them healed.

I knew God was real because I'd experienced him and even been healed, but I'd never seen healing happen through my own hands. I'd read many books about prayer and missionary stories, and I wondered *"Why does God always do great miracles for other people, and in other places, but not for me?"*

Then I went to a Christian conference called *"Healing Fusion."* I again encountered God in a powerful way. God showed me he had always wanted to do miracles for me, but that I lacked understanding. I began to comprehend the revelation of God's will as given through Christ. I began to see the significance of Jesus' coming in the flesh. After this, I laid my hands on many people and healing miracles started to happen.

I again felt God's goodness tangibly at that conference, like I had before. Over the next few years, as I studied, practiced, and meditated on these truths, this became a more regular and frequent experience.

There were periods of time for weeks where I felt like I was swimming in God's glory. It was as if the air around me became heavy with God's goodness, a little bit like water is when you move through it. I often felt currents love of flowing from my mouth and fingers. I jumped and shouted with joy.

Many times when I thought about passages of scripture, especially from Ephesians, Second Corinthians, or First John, it was like the air around me suddenly became electrified and I was overwhelmed with God's power. Thinking about certain scriptures and scriptural truths, as well as singing praise to God, seemed to *"trigger"* these experiences.

I have continued to find myself in need of God's present deliverance and salvation. I have had personal circumstances that caused me intense stress and anxiety. I've experienced grief. I have had to forgive. And I've felt anguish and distress over the suffering of people I love.

I have found myself in need of God's salvation again and again; and God has saved me again and again! In this, I don't refer to the assurance of being born again; as if I lost my place in God's family every time I blew it, thus needing to *"get saved"* again every time. I simply speak of God's present and ongoing deliverance in my life.

2 Corinthians 1:10 (NIV) He has delivered us from such a deadly peril, and he will deliver us again. On him we have set our hope that he will continue to deliver us

Heaven Itself

Christ's sacrifice did not only make the way for us to go to heaven when we die. It gave us present access to heaven! God made it possible for us to go to heaven now. This is salvation in the present, not only in the past or the future!

Maybe this sounds like a strange or mystical teaching. However if we understand it, we will see this clearly taught in scripture as a fundamental truth of the gospel!

It's amazing how books of the Bible that used to seem monotonous I now find so glorious! I still can't fathom how I once thought books like First and Second Corinthians were boring! I had to have been blind to not see the glory of the truth I was reading. Similarly, I'm astonished that I could have read Hebrews 9 and 10 so many times, yet missed what they say about our present access to heaven.

I don't remember exactly when it happened, but one day the Holy Spirit gave me understanding and I finally saw what it was saying! Since then, this truth has become one of the *"core values"* in my belief system. It has resulted in many miracles in my life. Let's look at it, starting in Hebrews chapter 9:

Hebrews 9:11-12, 22-26 (NIV) But when Christ came as high priest of the good things that are now already here, he went through the greater and more perfect tabernacle that is not made with human hands, that is to say, is not a part of this creation.

Chapter One—Present Access To Heaven

He did not enter by means of the blood of goats and calves; but he entered the Most Holy Place once for all by his own blood, thus obtaining eternal redemption…In fact, the law requires that nearly everything be cleansed with blood, and without the shedding of blood there is no forgiveness.

It was necessary, then, for the copies of the heavenly things to be purified with these sacrifices, but the heavenly things themselves with better sacrifices than these. For Christ did not enter a sanctuary made with human hands that was only a copy of the true one; he entered heaven itself, now to appear for us in God's presence.

Nor did he enter heaven to offer himself again and again, the way the high priest enters the Most Holy Place every year with blood that is not his own. Otherwise Christ would have had to suffer many times since the creation of the world. But he has appeared once for all at the culmination of the ages to do away with sin by the sacrifice of himself.

It is clear in Hebrews 9 that the Old Covenant tabernacle, the priest who entered once a year, and the thick veil separating the Holy Place from the Most Holy Place, were copies of heavenly things. Verse 24 says that Jesus entered heaven itself, which was the true Most Holy Place, to appear for us in God's presence. The Most Holy Place in the Old Covenant was only a copy; the real Most Holy Place is heaven itself!

Chapter 10 of Hebrews speaks of the supremacy of the heavenly realities and of the sacrifice of Christ, as compared to the copies of the realities—the tabernacle and sacrifices under the law. This passage tells us that the sacrifices under the law were an annual reminder of sin, but Christ's sacrifice removes sin. The sacrifices under the law were repeated, but Christ's sacrifice is once and for all.

Only the high priest could enter the Most Holy Place in the Old Covenant. But in this New Covenant, all of us who have been cleansed by Christ's sacrifice should have confidence to enter!

Hebrews 10:10, 14,19-22 (NIV) ... we have been made holy through the sacrifice of the body of Jesus Christ once for all... by one sacrifice he has made perfect forever those who are being made holy...

Therefore, brothers and sisters, since we have confidence to enter the Most Holy Place by the blood of Jesus, by a new and living way opened for us through the curtain, that is, his body, and since we have a great priest over the house of God, let us draw near to God with a sincere heart and with the full assurance that faith brings, having our hearts sprinkled to cleanse us from a guilty conscience and having our bodies washed with pure water.

The Most Holy Place we have confidence to enter is not that which was in place under the law, but is the true Most Holy Place, which Jesus entered; heaven itself! Verse 20 tells us that the way for us to enter the Most Holy Place is through the curtain, which is Jesus' body.

The Old Covenant tabernacle had a thick curtain which covered the Most Holy Place. Scripture tells us that when Jesus died, there was an earthquake and the curtain of the temple was torn in two.[4]

The curtain in the natural temple was torn as a sign that the way into the true Most Holy Place, heaven itself, was opened! We may enter heaven itself, now, through the body of Jesus which was torn for us.

---

[4] Matthew 27:51, Mark 15:38, Luke 23:45

Chapter One—Present Access To Heaven

Salvation is not only a thing that was accomplished in the past, giving us future access to heaven. Salvation is also present access to heaven; that which is available to us now!

2. God's Glory And Heaven
Heaven Is Where God Is

As discovered in the last chapter, we have access to the true Most Holy Place, which is heaven itself. To enter the Holiest Place and approach God's throne of grace is to enter heaven. Access to God's presence is access to heaven. The last verse in the book of Ezekiel describes the heavenly city as follows:

Ezekiel 48:35 "And the name of the city from that time on will be: THE LORD IS THERE."

The book of Hebrews also teaches us that we have come to this heavenly city. When we approach God, we enter heaven.

Hebrews 12:22-24 (NIV) But you have come to Mount Zion, to the city of the living God, the heavenly Jerusalem. You have come to thousands upon thousands of angels in joyful assembly, to the church of the firstborn, whose names are written in heaven. You have come to God, the Judge of all, to the spirits of the righteous made perfect, to Jesus the mediator of a new covenant, and to the sprinkled blood that speaks a better word than the blood of Abel.

Indeed, it is the presence and glory of God that makes heaven what it is. In 2 Corinthians 12, Paul talks about the *"third heaven"* and equates it with *"paradise."*

Present Access To Heaven

2 Corinthians 12:2-4 (NIV) I know a man in Christ who fourteen years ago was caught up to the third heaven. Whether it was in the body or out of the body I do not know—God knows. And I know that this man—whether in the body or apart from the body I do not know, but God knows—was caught up to paradise and heard inexpressible things.

The word *"paradise"* means *"God's garden"* or *"an Eden."*[5] This reminds us of the original garden of Eden, where Adam and Eve had access to the tree of life, and enjoyed unhindered fellowship with God.

Genesis 1:8-9, 15-17 (NIV) Now the Lord God had planted a garden in the east, in Eden; and there he put the man he had formed. The Lord God made all kinds of trees grow out of the ground—trees that were pleasing to the eye and good for food. In the middle of the garden were the tree of life and the tree of the knowledge of good and evil...
   The Lord God took the man and put him in the Garden of Eden to work it and take care of it. And the Lord God commanded the man, "You are free to eat from any tree in the garden; but you must not eat from the tree of the knowledge of good and evil, for when you eat from it you will certainly die."

So what was the tree of life, and how did man lose his place in paradise, or God's garden?

---

[5] Strong's Hebrew And Greek Dictionaries, Word G3857

Chapter Two—God's Glory And Heaven

The Tree Of Life

The tree of life was the tree of the knowledge of the Lord. This was opposed to the tree of the knowledge of good and evil, which brought death.

John 17:3 (NIV) Now this is eternal life: that they know you, the only true God, and Jesus Christ, whom you have sent.

There are different kinds of *"knowing."* What kind of *"knowledge"* of God is it that is eternal life? The same Greek word for *"know"*[6] is used in Ephesians chapter 3, describing a *"knowing"* that surpasses *"knowledge."* The Amplified Bible version of this gives a better understanding of the meaning.

Ephesians 3:19 (AMP) and [that you may come] to know [practically, through personal experience] the love of Christ which far surpasses [mere] knowledge [without experience], that you may be filled up [throughout your being] to all the fullness of God [so that you may have the richest experience of God's presence in your lives, completely filled and flooded with God Himself.]

Think of when the Bible says that *"Adam knew Eve, his wife; and she conceived."*[7] What kind of knowing was this? It was becoming one flesh with her! The Bible teaches that, in the same way, whoever is united to the Lord becomes one with him in spirit.[8] This is an experiential and participatory knowledge of the love of God.

---

[6] Strong's G1097
[7] Genesis 4:1 KJV
[8] 1 Corinthians 6:17

Love is the very essence of God's nature. The Apostle John wrote that *"God is love. Whoever lives in love lives in God, and God in him."*[9] The apostle Peter wrote about having such knowledge of the Lord that we become partakers in the divine nature.

2 Peter 1:1-4 Simeon Peter, a servant and apostle of Jesus Christ, To those who have received a faith as precious as ours through the righteousness of our God and Savior Jesus Christ: May grace and peace be yours in abundance in the knowledge of God and of Jesus our Lord.

His divine power has given us everything needed for life and godliness, through the knowledge of him who called us by his own glory and goodness. Thus he has given us, through these things, his precious and very great promises, so that through them you may escape from the corruption that is in the world because of lust, and may become participants of the divine nature.

Notice that it says grace and peace come in abundance through the *knowledge of God*, as well as *everything* we need for life and godliness. This is the same participatory and experiential knowledge of God, who is love, that John 17:3 speaks of. It is eternal life.

To experientially know the love of God that surpasses knowledge is not only to receive God's love. It is also to become love, as God is love. It is to become a participant in the divine nature. This is love perfected. The apostle John talked about *"perfect love."* Look carefully at these verses and how they fit together:

1 John 2:3-5 Now by this we may be sure that we know him, if we obey his commandments. Whoever says, "I

---

[9] 1 John 4:16, NIV

Chapter Two—God's Glory And Heaven

have come to know him," but does not obey his commandments, is a liar, and in such a person the truth does not exist; but whoever obeys his word, truly in this person the love of God has reached perfection.

1 John 4:12 No one has ever seen God; if we love one another, God lives in us, and his love is perfected in us.

John 15:9-12 As the Father has loved me, so I have loved you; abide in my love. If you keep my commandments, you will abide in my love, just as I have kept my Father's commandments and abide in his love. I have said these things to you so that my joy may be in you, and that your joy may be complete. "This is my commandment, that you love one another as I have loved you."

God's love reaches perfection in us when we obey his commandments, and his command is that we love one another as he has loved us. In other words, God's love has reached perfection in us when his love becomes our nature and we love as he does. This begins with receiving his love so that we can be transformed by it and give it to others.

The statement in John 15:9 is incredible and should strengthen every one of us. Jesus has loved us with the same love that Father God has for him! Later, in John 17:23, we read God the Father himself has loved us just as he loves Christ. The command to abide in God's love is not implying that we need to be good so that God will keep loving us, or else he will stop. No, God's love is a constant!

Rather, when we abide in God's love by loving as he loves, we are participating in the love of God. It is then that we fully receive all its benefits. When we do not participate in God's love by walking in it, God does not stop loving us, but we stop seeing God as he truly is.

We must give and receive the love of God. Look at the following verses

1 John 4:16-19 So we have known and believe the love that God has for us. God is love, and those who abide in love abide in God, and God abides in them. Love has been perfected among us in this: that we may have boldness on the day of judgment, because as he is, so are we in this world. There is no fear in love, but perfect love casts out fear; for fear has to do with punishment, and whoever fears has not reached perfection in love. We love because he first loved us.

1 John 3:2 What we do know is this: when he is revealed, we will be like him, for we will see him as he is.

Take a careful look at First John 4:17, where it says *"Love has been perfected among us in this." "This"* is referring to the previous verse, where it says that those who abide in love abide in God, and God abides in them.

The punctuation of some versions in English might make it a little confusing what *"this"* is referring to in verse 17. However, the Amplified version makes it clear by saying *"In this (union and fellowship with him), love is completed and perfected..."* It says here for the third time in First John that God's love is perfected in us when we love.

This is the perfect love that casts out fear: when we walk in love. As we experientially know the love of God, we become love and partake of the divine nature; we see the Lord as he is and become completely free from fear.

Seeing God's forgiveness as revealed through Christ sets us free from the fear of punishment. Being transformed by the love of God, so that we love others as he does, sets us free from the fear of what men can do to us. We aren't afraid of what can happen to us because we are no longer living for ourselves, but for others.

When we do not walk in love, God still loves us. His love is a constant. But we become blind, unable to see him as he truly is. Our view of God's nature becomes distorted. God still loves us, but we fail to abide in his love because we have become numb to it. First John teaches that we walk in light if we obey Jesus' new commandment to love each other as he has loved us; but if we do not, we walk in darkness.

1 John 2:8-9 (NIV) Yet I am writing you a new command; its truth is seen in him and in you, because the darkness is passing and the true light is already shining. Anyone who claims to be in the light but hates a brother or sister is still in the darkness. Anyone who loves their brother and sister lives in the light, and there is nothing in them to make them stumble. But anyone who hates a brother or sister is in the darkness and walks around in the darkness. They do not know where they are going, because the darkness has blinded them.

When we walk in darkness, we will walk in fear. Whoever fears has not been made perfect in love. God's love remains just as real and as wonderful. Yet if we do not participate in it by letting it transform us so that we love as God loves, we will walk in darkness and fear instead of in the knowledge of the Lord.

When we do not participate in God's love, we become blind and unable to see God as he truly is. When we walk in darkness, we are not abiding in the love that God has for us.

This gives us a new perspective on Hebrews 12:14, which says that *"without holiness no one will see the Lord."* (NIV) Sometimes holiness has been taught in a legalistic way. In reality, the scriptural truths about holiness are marvelous. Holiness is God's nature, all of which flows from his love.

Living in holiness is having the love of God fill and possess you so that you love like God loves. When you see God's holiness it is so wonderful and beautiful it makes you wholeheartedly want to be like him and to reflect his holiness to others.

So when I read that *"without holiness no one will see the Lord,"* it reminds me of the teaching of First John chapter 2, that the one who walks in love walks in light, but the one who does not love has become blind. Without holiness, you will not be able to see the Lord as he is; if you hate a brother or sister, the darkness blinds you.

If God's love (which is holiness) fills your heart, you walk in the light and there is nothing to make you stumble. When you walk in darkness, you are unable to experience the fullness of joy, the perfect peace that passes understanding and the freedom from fear that are found in God's presence.

Being blinded to the presence of the Lord is hell. To the degree that you walk in darkness, you will experience torment and hell on earth. As you see the Lord as he is and love as he loves, you will experience heaven's reality, even if your natural circumstances are difficult.

When scripture speaks of *"knowing God,"* of knowing the *"love of God that surpasses knowledge,"* and *"the knowledge of the glory of the Lord,"* these terms refer to the same concept and are interchangeable.

Knowing God is knowing the love of God, because God is love. To experientially know God's glory is to know his love. God's glory is the weightiness of his goodness and character of love. In the next book in this series, I write more about God's glory and the knowledge of his glory.

Chapter Two—God's Glory And Heaven

Truly, heaven is heaven because God is there and his nature of love permeates everything! There is no fear in heaven, because perfect love casts out fear. There is perfect peace, because the love of God reigns. There is fullness of joy, a joy unspeakable and full of glory, because of the presence of God who is love.

Psalm 16:11 You show me the path of life. In your presence there is fullness of joy; in your right hand are pleasures forevermore.

1 Peter 1:8 (KJV) Whom having not seen, ye love; in whom, though now ye see him not, yet believing, ye rejoice with joy unspeakable and full of glory

In the paradise of Eden, Adam and Eve had access to the tree of eternal life, which was the knowledge of the Lord. They experienced heavenly reality by participating in God's nature.

Revelation chapters 21 and 22 describe the heavenly Jerusalem which Hebrews 10:22 says that we have come to. The tree of life which was in Eden is described again as being in the heavenly city. This shows us that in the heavenly city men have been restored to partaking in God's nature, loving as God loves.

Revelation 22:1-2 Then the angel showed me the river of the water of life, bright as crystal, flowing from the throne of God and of the Lamb through the middle of the street of the city. On either side of the river is the tree of life with its twelve kinds of fruit, producing its fruit each month; and the leaves of the tree are for the healing of the nations.

The Tree Of The Knowledge Of Good And Evil

God told Adam and Even that if they ate the fruit of the tree of the knowledge of good and evil, they would surely die. When they ate the fruit of this tree, they sinned and fell short of the glory of God, as all of us have.[10] How did they sin? Satan tempted them by lying about God's nature and God's good intentions for them. When they acted upon the lie, their hearts became darkened.

To know God is to partake in his glory and his love, so that your nature is love. Adam and Eve's sin defiled their understanding of God. They became blind to the love of God and lost their true identity.

They could no longer esteem themselves as glorious beings, formed in the image and likeness of God. God created them to love, but by acting upon a lie, they took on a false identity. They took on an identity of sin and selfishness, enforced by guilt, shame, and fear.

As they lost their true identity they fell away from the knowledge of the Lord and of his love. They became blind to what God, in whose image they were created, was really like. Their view of God became distorted.

Romans 3:10-12 There is no one righteous, not even one; there is no one who understands; there is no one who seeks God. All have turned away, they have together become worthless; there is no one who does good, not even one.

Because eternal life is knowing God, the tree of life is the tree of the knowledge of the Lord. The knowledge of

---

[10] Romans 3:23

Chapter Two—God's Glory And Heaven

the Lord is the essence of heaven. When man sinned, he chose not to retain the knowledge of the Lord.

This is why Adam and Eve were removed from God's garden (Paradise). Heaven is no longer heaven if love does not reign. The book of Romans describes the blindness that comes from refusing to retain the knowledge of the Lord:

Romans 1:21, 28-31 (NIV) For although they knew God, they neither glorified him as God nor gave thanks to him, but their thinking became futile and their foolish hearts were darkened.... Furthermore, just as they did not think it worthwhile to retain the knowledge of God, so God gave them over to a depraved mind, so that they do what ought not to be done.

They have become filled with every kind of wickedness, evil, greed and depravity. They are full of envy, murder, strife, deceit and malice. They are gossips, slanderers, God-haters, insolent, arrogant and boastful; they invent ways of doing evil; they disobey their parents; they have no understanding, no fidelity, no love, no mercy.

Just as men became depraved when they did not retain the knowledge of God, it is through the knowledge of the Lord that we escape the defilements of the world:

2 Peter 2:20 For if, after they have escaped the defilements of the world through the knowledge of our Lord and Savior Jesus Christ, they are again entangled in them and overpowered, the last state has become worse for them than the first.

Rick Joyner wrote a book called *"There Were Two Trees In The Garden."*[11] He noted the tree that brings death is not called *"the tree of evil,"* but *"the tree of the knowledge of good and evil."* There is a *"good"* side to the tree that brings death.

It's not a *"good"* which flows out of love and unhindered fellowship with the Lord. It is a humanistic *"good,"* motivated by pride, guilt, and self-centeredness. *"Good"* motivated by guilt is good that is done to try to make up for past failures.

"Good" motivated by pride and self-centeredness is good done out of a desire to measure up, and not out of genuine love for others. It's not the same *"good"* that comes naturally for those who know God. Rather, it's a self-righteousness that can never compare to God's righteousness.

Isaiah 64:4 (NIV) "...and all our righteous acts are like filthy rags"

Guilt is a sin identity, whereas true righteousness is the identity that comes from knowing God. Did you ever sin again and again, continuing to try to do better, to be better, to change yourself? Did it ever bring life to you or to anyone else?

No, because whatever *"good"* you did, was motivated by self-centeredness, guilt, and shame. It was still coming from a sin identity. Self-righteousness is our self-centered attempt at being *"good,"* motivated by guilt and shame. This is opposed to God's righteousness, which is a *"good"* that flows from a participatory knowledge of the love of God.

---

[11] Joyner, Rick. *There Were Two Trees In The Garden.* Charlotte, NC: Morning Star Publications, 1986, 1990, 1992, 1992

Chapter Two—God's Glory And Heaven

When we walk in God's righteousness, we do good because we see God as he is and are like him.[12] Just as God is love, so are we.

    This is why guilt had to be dealt with. As long as there was guilt and shame, they formed a self-centered sin-identity in us. Therefore, any *"good"* that we could do would only end up bringing death because it was not rooted in the knowledge of the Lord, the tree of life. This was why Jesus' sacrifice was necessary.

Hebrews 9:22 Indeed, under the law almost everything is purified with blood, and without the shedding of blood there is no forgiveness of sins.

This is the mystery of the atonement: Jesus had to die to deal with guilt so that we could be restored to the knowledge of the Lord and see God as he truly is. He bore our sin[13] and also took on himself the death and destruction that were the fruit of our sin.[14]

    Guilt and shame made it impossible to know and understand God's nature by experience. As long as they weren't dealt with, we could never see God as he is, and so neither would we partake of the fruit of the tree of life by becoming participants in his nature.

    I don't fully understand how Jesus' atonement works, but I know it does work. I know that it deals with guilt and reveals God's love to us so that we can see what God is really like.

Romans 3:23 But God proves his love for us in that while we still were sinners Christ died for us.

---

[12] 1 John 3:2
[13] Isaiah 53:6, 12
[14] Isaiah 53:5

1 John 4:9-10 God's love was revealed among us in this way: God sent his only Son into the world so that we might live through him. In this is love, not that we loved God but that he loved us and sent his Son to be the atoning sacrifice for our sins.

1 John 4:19 We love because he first loved us.

1 John 3:16 We know love by this, that he laid down his life for us—and we ought to lay down our lives for one another.

I've stated that love is perfected when we become love. To become love, we must first receive the love of God. When I saw how Jesus suffered and died for me, I saw the love of God, and that love transformed me.

When I believed that Jesus took my guilt and sin upon himself, I gained a new identity; no longer defined by guilt but by the love of God. I ate of the tree of life, the knowledge of the Lord! This is how Jesus' death on the cross brings us into eternal life. It enables us to know the Father; to both receive God's love and to become a participant in his nature of love.

2 Corinthians 5:21 For our sake he made him to be sin who knew no sin, so that in him we might become the righteousness of God.

The fall was man refusing to retain the knowledge of God. As a result mankind become spiritually blind and could no longer see Him as he truly is.

Salvation is having our eyes opened to see the light of the glory of God in the face of Christ. Salvation is being able to once again see God as he is; receiving his love and becoming like him. Salvation is coming into the knowledge of his glory.

Chapter Two—God's Glory And Heaven

2 Corinthians 4:3-6 And even if our gospel is veiled, it is veiled to those who are perishing. The god of this age has blinded the minds of unbelievers, so that they cannot see the light of the gospel that displays the glory of Christ, who is the image of God.

For what we preach is not ourselves, but Jesus Christ as Lord, and ourselves as your servants for Jesus' sake. For God, who said, "Let light shine out of darkness," made his light shine in our hearts to give us the light of the knowledge of God's glory displayed in the face of Christ.

Men were kicked out of God's garden, Paradise, at the fall. They were denied access to eating the fruit of the tree of life, which is knowing God: eternal life. Salvation is Paradise restored.

Because of what Jesus accomplished on the cross, we can know God and again partake of the tree of life. We don't have to wait until we die to go to heaven and eat its fruit! We can see God as he is, receive his love, and become love like He is love, participating in his divine nature.

Jesus' teaching confirms that the one who believes in him has access to the tree of life. Just as those who ate the fruit of the tree of life would never die, Jesus taught that the one who believed on him and ate of his flesh would live forever:

John 6:47-51 Very truly, I tell you, whoever believes has eternal life. I am the bread of life. Your ancestors ate the manna in the wilderness, and they died. This is the bread that comes down from heaven, so that one may eat of it and not die. I am the living bread that came down from heaven. Whoever eats of this bread will live forever; and

Present Access To Heaven

the bread that I will give for the life of the world is my flesh.

3. Growing In The Knowledge Of The Lord

Present Heavenly Realities Accessible Through The Gospel

We must grow in our understanding of what the gospel implies and makes possible in the present. Much more is possible right now than we have ever experienced before.

Evangelicalism has emphasized the past aspect of salvation, which is important. We who have put our faith in Christ have been born again. We have been forgiven; we have been adopted; we have been given new hearts; we are new creations in Christ; and we have been accepted into God's family.

However, so many Christians lack joy and peace! So many have been bought by Christ's blood, yet are in bondage to fear. So many believers are depressed and worried. So many are bound by addiction and sin, and do not experience the freedom that Christ purchased for them with his blood!

How many believers do you know who overflow with the love of God so much that their faces are radiant and when others see them, they see Jesus? How many constantly have such virtue flowing from their beings, that all who touch them are healed, just as all who touched Jesus were healed?

How many Christians do you know who overflow with joy and the love of God in the worst of situations, as did Betsie Ten Boom in a Nazi concentration camp? How many believers can simply walk into a place and people all around weep in repentance because they see the glory of God, as happened around the 19th century revivalist Charles Finney and others such as Smith Wigglesworth?

You may see *"exceptional"* Christians such as these and think you could never be like them. I remind you that they were people like we are, with similar weaknesses. The Bible says this very thing about the mighty prophet Elijah, who challenged the prophets of Baal and turned a nation back to God. He was a man like us.[15]

What Spirit dwells in you if you are born again? Is it not the very Spirit of the Living God? Is there anything that he cannot do? Is there anything that is too hard for him? Can the same Holy Spirit who raised Christ from the dead not turn your weakness into strength? If you feel like a wimp, can he not make you into a warrior, so that you will say *"With my God I can crush a troop? With him I can leap over a wall?"*[16]

The Holy Spirit can do everything that you cannot do! Now if God has not withheld his own Son, Jesus, from you, will he withhold anything?[17] Does not the Bible say that God has predestined you to be conformed to the image of his Son, Jesus?[18] Is this too hard for the Holy Spirit to do? No, God is able to do abundantly more than you could ever ask or imagine, according to his power that is at work within you![19] Nothing is too hard for Him!

---

[15] James 5:17
[16] Psalm 18:29
[17] Romans 8:32
[18] Romans 8:29
[19] Ephesians 3:20

Chapter Three—Growing In The Knowledge Of The Lord

Has God not promised that he will be with you? He will help you and uphold you with his glorious right hand;[20] he will answer you when you call;[21] he will never leave you or forsake you;[22] and he will be faithful to complete the work that he began in you.[23] If God is with you, who can be against you?[24]

I encourage you to see what the Holy Spirit can do in you and to embrace his work with all your heart. Let the Holy Spirit touch every part of your being. Let him make you into a person who walks on earth and yet lives in heavenly reality at the same time. He will help you to forgive when you cannot forgive. When you feel like you can no longer love, his love will fill you and lift you. This is why God has given you his Holy Spirit.

If you belong to Christ, you have been born again and God has given you the Holy Spirit. Scripture says that whoever unites himself with the Lord becomes one with him in Spirit.[25] The Holy Spirit dwells within you to strengthen your spirit; to do his work in and through you. The life of God is at work in you! I thank God for what he is doing in you and what he will do. I bless the work of the Holy Spirit in your life.

Christians too often get used to living in so much less than all that is made possible through the gospel. We forget how wonderful the gospel is and how glorious the promises of God in Christ are. We think as if all we have experienced is all that there is, doubting the awesomeness of God's promises.

---

[20] Isaiah 41:10
[21] Psalm 50:15, Jeremiah 33:3
[22] Hebrews 13:5
[23] Philippians 1:6
[24] Romans 8:31
[25] 1 Corinthians 6:17

Present Access To Heaven

We forget that Father God loves us with the same love that he has for Jesus[26] and that he has given us the same glory that he gave to Jesus![27] We fail to remember that Jesus is not ashamed to call us his brothers![28] Consider again the following passage of scripture:

Ephesians 3:14-21 (NIV) For this reason I kneel before the Father, from whom every family in heaven and on earth derives its name. I pray that out of his glorious riches he may strengthen you with power through his Spirit in your inner being, so that Christ may dwell in your hearts through faith. And I pray that you, being rooted and established in love, may have power, together with all the Lord's holy people, to grasp how wide and long and high and deep is the love of Christ, and to know this love that surpasses knowledge—that you may be filled to the measure of all the fullness of God.

Now to him who is able to do immeasurably more than all we ask or imagine, according to his power that is at work within us, to him be glory in the church and in Christ Jesus throughout all generations, for ever and ever! Amen.

What would it look like for you to be *"filled to the measure of all the fullness of God?"* This is God's aim for you! God's purpose is to conform you to the image of Christ,[29] in whom all the fullness of God dwells.[30]

I want to remind you of God's promises and of what is possible for you now in Christ, so that you settle for nothing less than all he has provided for you in the gospel.

---

[26] John 17:23
[27] John 17:22
[28] Hebrews 2:11
[29] Romans 8:29
[30] Colossians 2:9

Chapter Three—Growing In The Knowledge Of The Lord

Continuing In Our Salvation

We just read Paul's prayer that believers would know the love of God that surpasses knowledge, thus being filled to the measure of all the fullness of God. This is interesting when compared to what Paul wrote in Colossians:

Colossians 2:6-10 As you therefore have received Christ Jesus the Lord, continue to live your lives in him, rooted and built up in him and established in the faith, just as you were taught, abounding in thanksgiving.

See to it that no one takes you captive through philosophy and empty deceit, according to human tradition, according to the elemental spirits of the universe, and not according to Christ. For in him the whole fullness of deity dwells bodily, and you have come to fullness in him, who is the head of every ruler and authority.

We read here that we have already been given fullness in Christ. It is true. Jesus did not withhold anything, but has made known to us all that the Father revealed to him,[31] he has loved us with the same love the Father has for him,[32] and has given us the same glory that the Father gave to him.[33]

We have been given fullness in Christ, but that fullness fills every part of our being only as we come to *"know the love of God that surpasses knowledge."* As that happens, the fullness of God which we were given when we received the Holy Spirit floods and fills our souls, bodies, emotions, and every part of our being.

---

[31] John 15:15
[32] John 17:22
[33] John 15:9

Verse 6 says that as we received Christ, we must continue to live in him. This *"being rooted and built up in Christ"* and *"established in the faith,"* is salvation in the present. This is why we need to hold fast to the truth of the gospel.

Though I don't imply that we *"lose"* our salvation when we don't hold fast to the simple truth of the gospel, we become accustomed to living in much less than all that is provided in salvation. It becomes our *"normal,"* even though it should be subnormal.

A person is vaccinated by receiving a dead or weakened version of a virus in order to make him resistant to it. Satan, the father of lies,[34] works to undermine and weaken our understanding of the gospel, so that we become resistant to it. This is why we must hold fast to truth and be established in the faith, as Colossians teaches.

Ephesians says that it is when we *"know the love of God that surpasses knowledge"* that we are filled with all the fullness of God. This is a repeated theme in scripture. We are growing in the knowledge of the Lord. As we do so, beholding God's glory in the face of Christ,[35] we are transformed and go from one degree of glory to another.

Colossians 1:10 ...so that you may lead lives worthy of the Lord, fully pleasing to him, as you bear fruit in every good work and as you grow in the knowledge of God.

2 Peter 3:18 But grow in the grace and knowledge of our Lord and Savior Jesus Christ. To him be the glory both now and to the day of eternity. Amen.

---

[34] John 8:44
[35] 2 Corinthians 4:6

Chapter Three—Growing In The Knowledge Of The Lord

2 Corinthians 3:7-18 Now if the ministry of death, chiseled in letters on stone tablets, came in glory so that the people of Israel could not gaze at Moses' face because of the glory of his face, a glory now set aside, how much more will the ministry of the Spirit come in glory? For if there was glory in the ministry of condemnation, much more does the ministry of justification abound in glory! Indeed, what once had glory has lost its glory because of the greater glory; for if what was set aside came through glory, much more has the permanent come in glory!

Since, then, we have such a hope, we act with great boldness, not like Moses, who put a veil over his face to keep the people of Israel from gazing at the end of the glory that was being set aside. But their minds were hardened. Indeed, to this very day, when they hear the reading of the old covenant, that same veil is still there, since only in Christ is it set aside.

Indeed, to this very day whenever Moses is read, a veil lies over their minds; but when one turns to the Lord, the veil is removed. Now the Lord is the Spirit, and where the Spirit of the Lord is, there is freedom. And all of us, with unveiled faces, seeing the glory of the Lord as though reflected in a mirror, are being transformed into the same image from one degree of glory to another; for this comes from the Lord, the Spirit.

Growing in the knowledge of the Lord and being transformed as we behold his glory are how we are *"being saved."* This is salvation in the present. So how do we grow in the knowledge of the Lord?

How did we first enter this restoration to the experiential knowledge of the Lord? How did we first behold his glory, his love? We looked to Christ. When we saw him dying on the cross, we understood that God proved his love for us in that while we were still sinners,

Christ died for us.[36] When we saw the love of Jesus towards even his enemies, we saw what God is really like.

We also saw that our sin identity died with him and we were raised with him in newness of life; in the likeness of God, with a love nature. The guilt was removed so that we could become partakers in the divine nature. [37]

In the same way that we were born again and came into this knowledge of the Lord (past salvation), we grow in the knowledge of the Lord (present salvation). As Colossians 2:6 teaches, we continue to live in Christ just as we received him.

We continue to hold fast to the truth of the gospel and let the revelation of the love of God continue to transform us. As we continue to look to the Lord, the veils are removed. Veils are things that hinder us from seeing God as he truly is.

The Passion Play

I have never gotten tired of hearing the message of the gospel. I remember when it became alive to me, when I was a kid. It felt like heaven. The place was electric with the goodness of God. There was such joy in receiving his forgiveness, such love revealed!

As a young Christian who struggled with condemnation, for a while I felt like I had to *"get saved"* again every time I heard the gospel. I had not yet learned to hold fast to the truth of what Christ had done. As I grew in the Lord, I became confident in the work God had done in me. I was delivered from this *"veil"* of condemning lies that kept me from experiencing the love and joy I had the first time the gospel became real to me.

---

[36] Romans 5:8
[37] 2 Peter 1:4

Chapter Three—Growing In The Knowledge Of The Lord

Every time I am reminded of what Jesus did for me, I experience God's love in a fresh way. I no longer feel like I need to *"get saved"* or be forgiven again, but I do let the love that was revealed in Christ's death and the power that was revealed in his resurrection continue to transform me.

I remember the *"new and living way"* that Jesus made when his body was torn, so that I could enter the Holiest Place, heaven itself. I enter heaven and behold God's glory; and so I am growing in the knowledge of God and going from one degree of glory to another as I behold his glory.

The church I attended for many years showed a film of the death and resurrection of Christ on Valentine's Day, and did a passion play near Easter. I shed many tears as I was reminded of the love that compelled Jesus to say, *"Father, forgive them, for they know not what they do."*

I felt my heart soften and overflow with love again as I beheld the glory of God in the face of Jesus. Being reminded of how Jesus revealed God's love through his life and death, I forgave others who had wronged me and felt a weight lift off of my shoulders.

As I saw God's love again, I experienced heaven. Once again, I knew a love that filled my being to overflowing, casting out fear; peace that passes understanding; and joy unspeakable and full of glory. I literally jumped and shouted again with the joy of salvation.

This is the reason that Jesus commanded us to take communion in remembrance of him. Christians need to be reminded again and again of the message of the gospel, not because we need to *"get saved"* again anytime we stumble, but because we need to hold fast to the truth of the gospel and let the revelation of God's love continue to transform us. When we do this, we learn to count ourselves as dead to sin and alive to righteousness.[38]

I played the part of Jesus in the passion play several times. It was difficult to look at all those people hating me and torturing me, and say, with love in my eyes *"Father, forgive them, for they know not what they do."* It was hard to feel the depths of Christ's love for these people as I said this. But to be a good portrayal of Jesus in the skit, I had to try to feel the love that Jesus felt as he said this.

Practicing again and again caused me to focus on the love that Christ showed as he died. It broke me and made my heart soft and tender. If there was any hardness or unforgiveness in me, it melted away. I saw again what God was really like. My revelation of his love became fresh all over again. I truly experienced a heavenly glory that no words could describe. I did not even want to speak for a time because I was so in awe of God's love.

I remember once when my mother and sister also acted in the skit. They wept at the foot of the cross. It seemed so real that my little cousin thought the crucifixion was currently happening. She believed they were torturing me and I was actually dying, and she was bawling!

Everyone had to comfort her and explain to her that it was only a skit. Our emotions were deeply impacted with the extremity of what Jesus did. It wasn't just a story; it was a reality! Our mental understanding became more of a heart understanding.

Richard Wurmbrand recounted his experience of preaching the gospel to a Russian officer. This officer loved and longed for God, but knew nothing about him. He had never seen a bible.

---

[38] Romans 6:11

Chapter Three—Growing In The Knowledge Of The Lord

When Wurmbrand read the Sermon on the Mount and Jesus' parables to the officer, he danced around the room saying *"What a wonderful beauty! How could I live without knowing this Christ?"* Wurmbrand had never seen a person with such joy in the Lord.

Then Wurmbrand read about Jesus' passion and crucifixion. When this Russian officer heard of Jesus' death, he fell in a chair and wept bitterly. He thought the Savior he had just heard of was dead! He hadn't yet heard of Jesus' resurrection.

When he heard of the resurrection, he swore, using what Wurmbrand called *"very dirty, but very 'holy' profanity."* Then he danced around the room in ecstasy shouting *"He's alive! He's alive!"*[39]

Wurmbrand said preaching the gospel to Russians is heaven on earth. He was right. The gospel truly is heaven on earth if it is understood.

At the end of one passion play, I walked down the aisle of the church as the resurrected Jesus. I felt the love and the joy of the Lord explode from my heart. What Jesus had done was absolutely real to me. It seemed as if every cell of my body was filled with the life of God. I wanted nothing more than to represent this love that Jesus showed to others. It really did feel like my face was glowing.

A little girl who was very dear to me was there. She was four or five years old, and had been having stomach pain and feeling sick during the whole meeting. When she saw Jesus, in the skit, coming out of the grave in resurrection glory, she was instantly healed. God's love overwhelmed me all the more as I heard this little

---

[39] Wurmbrand, Richard (2010-09-30). Tortured for Christ (Kindle Locations 304-330). Living Sacrifice Book Company. Kindle Edition.

girl tell us what happened to her when she saw Jesus walking down the aisle with outstretched arms.

This is why the gospel needs to be preached to Christians. In it is God's saving power for all who believe.[40] Just as we first came to salvation through believing the gospel, we experience the glorious present realities of salvation by continuing in the truth of the gospel.

We experience heaven now by holding fast to the truth of the gospel. If we lack the present experience of God's power and presence, (including the same peace, joy, and freedom from fear that are found in heaven) we must ask ourselves if we have held fast to the truth of the gospel. If not, we have been seduced into denying some of its realities without realizing it.

The Full Measure Of The Stature Of Christ

In past salvation, we were raised with Christ in newness of life [41] and given a new spirit, created in the likeness of God in true righteousness and holiness.[42] In present salvation, we are growing in the knowledge of the Lord,[43] being transformed by the renewing of our minds,[44] so that the life of Christ which God has planted in us fills our minds, souls, and bodies — every part of our being — until we all come to maturity, to the full measure of the stature of Christ.

Notice again the phrase *"the knowledge of the Son of God,"* in Ephesians 4:13. The concept of the *"knowledge of the Lord"* is a major theme in scripture. It's found again and again.

---

[40] Romans 1:16
[41] Romans 6:4
[42] Ephesians 4:24
[43] Colossians 1:10
[44] Romans 12:2

Chapter Three—Growing In The Knowledge Of The Lord

Ephesians 4:13 until all of us come to the unity of the faith and of the knowledge of the Son of God, to maturity, to the measure of the full stature of Christ.

When the church, which is the body of Christ, grows into the full measure of the stature of Christ, then we will do what Jesus did. If all who touched Jesus were healed, everyone who we touch will be healed. Jesus said that we would do the same works as he did, and even greater works. [45]

We must remind ourselves that Jesus said he gave us the same glory which the Father gave him.[46] Yet we mature to reach the stature of Christ in all things as we behold the glory of God in the face of Jesus and are transformed into the same image, growing in the knowledge of the Lord.

2 Corinthians 4:6 For it is the God who said, "Let light shine out of darkness," who has shone in our hearts to give the light of the knowledge of the glory of God in the face of Jesus Christ.

As the body of Christ, God has given us the same authority as Jesus exercised. Jesus, the man of heaven, exercised the dominion of heaven to bring the reality of heaven to people around him. We are to do the same.

Jesus said *"As the Father has sent me, I send you."*[47] What do we do if we don't yet see something in subjection which we have been given dominion over? We keep looking to Jesus. As we behold him we experience heaven now and are transformed so that we think, speak, and act as heavenly people. As we grow in

---

[45] John 14:12
[46] John 17:22
[47] John 20:21

the knowledge of the Lord we will increasingly exercise the dominion of heaven on the earth.

4. Removing The Veils
What Are Veils?

Jesus triumphed over Satan at the cross, disarming him,[48] and rescuing us from his power.[49] He also gave us authority to tread upon all the power of the enemy.[50] The way that Satan keeps oppressing people is through lies. He is a liar and the father of lies.[51]

Just as Satan tempted Adam and Eve to doubt God's nature, so he is always speaking lies in order to distort or darken people's view of God. He also lies to us who are born-again so that we would doubt the truth of the Gospel, through which we partake of the knowledge of the Lord, which is eating from the tree of life.

When a Christian believes the enemy's lies he becomes subject to feelings of guilt and condemnation and can come under oppression in various ways. It is not that God has withdrawn forgiveness, or that the believer is no longer a new creation.[52] Although he has been born again, he is not presently experiencing the fullness of all that salvation encompasses. This fullness includes everything that is in heaven.

We read earlier from 2 Corinthians 3 about being transformed by beholding the glory of the Lord. Let's look at part of that passage again:

---

[48] Colossians 2:14
[49] Colossians 1:13
[50] Luke 10:19
[51] John 8:44
[52] 2 Corinthians 5:17

Present Access To Heaven

2 Corinthians 3:12-18 Since, then, we have such a hope, we act with great boldness, not like Moses, who put a veil over his face to keep the people of Israel from gazing at the end of the glory that was being set aside. But their minds were hardened. Indeed, to this very day, when they hear the reading of the old covenant, that same veil is still there, since only in Christ is it set aside. Indeed, to this very day whenever Moses is read, a veil lies over their minds; but when one turns to the Lord, the veil is removed.

Now the Lord is the Spirit, and where the Spirit of the Lord is, there is freedom. And all of us, with unveiled faces, seeing the glory of the Lord as though reflected in a mirror, are being transformed into the same image from one degree of glory to another; for this comes from the Lord, the Spirit.

In this passage, we read about minds being hardened. This is the blindness that scripture refers to, which keeps people from seeing the light of the glory of God. As we will talk about in the next book, it is the *"thick darkness that covers the peoples."*[53] Note that only in Christ is it set aside. It is only through Christ that we can be restored to an experiential knowledge of the Lord's glory and eat the fruit of the tree of life. There's no other way.

In this scripture the *"veil"* that was keeping people from seeing God was the law of the Old Covenant. However, anything that keeps us from seeing the Lord as he is can be a veil. The good news is that as we continually look to the Lord, the veils are removed and we grow in the knowledge of the Lord.

As this happens we become filled with all the fullness of God. We become heavenly people, living and

---

[53] Isaiah 60:2

walking in the reality of heaven even though we are on earth, because we are walking in the light of the Lord's glory.

When the church grows into the full measure of Christ's stature, being filled with all the fullness of God, then the earth will become like heaven, because the knowledge of God's glory will fill the earth as the waters cover the seas.[54]

When I saw these truths, a militant desire arose in my heart to not shrink back, but to learn to walk on this earth as a man of heaven, and to learn to make everywhere I go like heaven. I saw that as I looked to the Lord the veils would be removed, and that I must destroy arguments and every proud obstacle raised up against the knowledge of God.

2 Corinthians 10:3-5 Indeed, we live as human beings, but we do not wage war according to human standards; for the weapons of our warfare are not merely human, but they have divine power to destroy strongholds. We destroy arguments and every proud obstacle raised up against the knowledge of God, and we take every thought captive to obey Christ.

We grow in the knowledge of the Lord as these lies which obscured our view of God are destroyed. Knowing God and being filled with his fullness is more important than anything else.

Philippians 3:8 I regard everything as loss because of the surpassing value of knowing Christ Jesus my Lord. For his sake I have suffered the loss of all things, and I regard them as rubbish, in order that I may gain Christ.

---

[54] Habakkuk 2:14

What are some of these veils, arguments, and proud obstacles which are raised up against the knowledge of the Lord? Let's look at a few of them.

The Old Covenant Law

The veil that 2 Corinthians 3 speaks of is the Old Covenant law that was done away with. The law was good,[55] but it was powerless to justify us[56] or bring us into the knowledge of the Lord; through it came the knowledge of sin,[57] and not of righteousness. Since the law did not lead to the knowledge of the Lord, but to the knowledge of sin, it was from the *"good"* part of the tree of the knowledge of good and evil.

Just like the fruit of the tree of the knowledge of good and evil did, the law brought death.[58] Rather than freeing from sin, the law caused sin to multiply,[59] aroused our sinful passions,[60] and revived sin.[61] The law was flawed,[62] and perfection was simply not attainable through it.[63]

The old law was abolished[64] and became obsolete[65] because it was weak and ineffectual,[66] and a better hope was introduced, through which we may now approach God[67] and enter heaven itself.[68] This was a new

---

[55] Romans 7:12, 16
[56] Galatians 2:16, 3:11
[57] Romans 3:20
[58] Romans 7:5, 9-10, Romans 8:2, 1 Corinthians 15:56,
[59] Romans 5:20
[60] Romans 7:5
[61] Romans 7:9
[62] Hebrews 8:7
[63] Hebrews 7:11+19, 10:1
[64] Ephesians 2:15
[65] Hebrews 8:13
[66] Hebrews 7:18
[67] Hebrews 7:19
[68] Hebrews 9:24, 10:19

Chapter Four—Removing The Veils

law, the law of the Spirit of life in Christ,[69] the Spirit of God dwelling in man; the knowledge of the Lord.

This law of life was not in letter, but was written on our hearts by the Spirit of God. Unlike the old law which was of the tree of the knowledge of good and evil, this law was the knowledge of the Lord which was made possible through the forgiveness of sins. Under this new commandment, we love as God loves, because we have received God's love and that love has become our nature.

Jeremiah 31:31-34 The days are surely coming, says the LORD, when I will make a new covenant with the house of Israel and the house of Judah. It will not be like the covenant that I made with their ancestors when I took them by the hand to bring them out of the land of Egypt—a covenant that they broke, though I was their husband, says the LORD.

But this is the covenant that I will make with the house of Israel after those days, says the LORD: I will put my law within them, and I will write it on their hearts; and I will be their God, and they shall be my people. No longer shall they teach one another, or say to each other, "Know the LORD," for they shall all know me, from the least of them to the greatest, says the LORD; for I will forgive their iniquity, and remember their sin no more.

2 Corinthians 3:5-6 Not that we are competent of ourselves to claim anything as coming from us; our competence is from God, who has made us competent to be ministers of a new covenant, not of letter but of spirit; for the letter kills, but the Spirit gives life.

We had to die to the old law, which was of the tree of the knowledge of good and evil, to live in the new law, the

---

[69] Romans 8:2

knowledge of the Lord. This knowledge of the Lord comes by justification through grace[70] and produces grace.[71]

This law, of the knowledge of the Lord through grace, is Christ's new commandment that we love as he loves us.[72] This law empowers us. This is the law of righteousness and of being led by the Spirit of God. Let's look at some scriptures which contrast the law of the old covenant with the new law of grace and righteousness which we have received:

Romans 6:14 For sin will have no dominion over you, since you are not under law but under grace.

Romans 7:4 In the same way, my friends, you have died to the law through the body of Christ, so that you may belong to another, to him who has been raised from the dead in order that we may bear fruit for God.

Romans 10:4 For Christ is the end of the law so that there may be righteousness for everyone who believes.

Galatians 5:18 But if you are led by the Spirit, you are not subject to the law.

One reason Christians presently experience much less than heaven's reality, struggling with sin and lacking in power, is that they have been bewitched into following the old law that is in letter but not in the knowledge of the Lord through grace. Just as we first received salvation through grace, we must continue in it by grace.

---

[70] Romans 3:24, Titus 3:7
[71] 2 Peter 1:2
[72] John 13:34

Galatians 3:1-5 You foolish Galatians! Who has bewitched you? It was before your eyes that Jesus Christ was publicly exhibited as crucified! The only thing I want to learn from you is this: Did you receive the Spirit by doing the works of the law or by believing what you heard? Are you so foolish? Having started with the Spirit, are you now ending with the flesh? Did you experience so much for nothing?—if it really was for nothing. Well then, does God supply you with the Spirit and work miracles among you by your doing the works of the law, or by your believing what you heard?

Galatians 3:10 For all who rely on the works of the law are under a curse…

Galatians 5:4 You who want to be justified by the law have cut yourselves off from Christ; you have fallen away from grace.

The power of God unto salvation is in the message of the gospel.[73] If we are really believing the gospel, God's power and miracles should manifest abundantly among us. One of the main reasons that many are lacking in the manifestation of the Holy Spirit and don't see miracles is that they are trying to attain them through the works of the law instead of by simply believing the gospel.

Sin, Guilt, And Shame

2 Corinthians 5:17-21 So if anyone is in Christ, there is a new creation: everything old has passed away; see, everything has become new! All this is from God, who reconciled us to himself through Christ, and has given us the ministry of reconciliation; that is, in Christ God was reconciling the world to himself, not counting their

---

[73] Romans 1:16

trespasses against them, and entrusting the message of reconciliation to us.

So we are ambassadors for Christ, since God is making his appeal through us; we entreat you on behalf of Christ, be reconciled to God. For our sake he made him to be sin who knew no sin, so that in him we might become the righteousness of God.

Scripture teaches that Jesus took on our sin identity and died with it. We died with Christ to the sin identity and were resurrected with him in newness of life, with an identity of righteousness. Our new identity is created in the likeness of God, in true righteousness and holiness. It is our new nature to love like God loves; to be holy as He is holy.

Yet our adversary, the *"accuser of the brethren,"*[74] continues to accuse and lie to believers, telling us we are sinners. We are not unaware of his schemes.[75] He speaks lies and tries to get us to think they are our own thoughts. He tempts us and tries to get us to think the temptation comes from our own minds; that we have sinned just by having the thought. He wants us to believe we are still sinners. If we do sin, he bombards us with accusation and condemnation.

Since we are made in God's image, our view of God becomes distorted when our view of ourselves is distorted. Satan's lying accusations that we are still sinners are some of these *"arguments"* that are raised up against the knowledge of the Lord. When we walk in the righteousness that we have been given, God's love nature, we walk in the light and will see the Lord as he truly is.

---

[74] Revelation 12:10
[75] 2 Corinthians 2:11 NIV

Chapter Four—Removing The Veils

1 John 1:5-7 This is the message we have heard from him and proclaim to you, that God is light and in him there is no darkness at all. If we say that we have fellowship with him while we are walking in darkness, we lie and do not do what is true; but if we walk in the light as he himself is in the light, we have fellowship with one another, and the blood of Jesus his Son cleanses us from all sin.

1 John 2:10 Whoever loves a brother or sister lives in the light, and in such a person there is no cause for stumbling.

When Satan comes with his lying accusations, we learn to stand on the truth and remind him that our old sin identity died with Christ. We consider ourselves dead to sin and alive to God in Jesus, receiving God's free gift of righteousness.[76] We throw aside everything that would darken our understanding or hinder us from seeing the Lord as he is.

Romans 6:1-4, 11 What then are we to say? Should we continue in sin in order that grace may abound? By no means! How can we who died to sin go on living in it? Do you not know that all of us who have been baptized into Christ Jesus were baptized into his death? Therefore we have been buried with him by baptism into death, so that, just as Christ was raised from the dead by the glory of the Father, so we too might walk in newness of life. So you also must consider yourselves dead to sin and alive to God in Christ Jesus.

Ephesians 4:17-24 Now this I affirm and insist on in the Lord: you must no longer live as the Gentiles live, in the

---

[76] Romans 5:17

futility of their minds. They are darkened in their understanding, alienated from the life of God because of their ignorance and hardness of heart. They have lost all sensitivity and have abandoned themselves to licentiousness, greedy to practice every kind of impurity.
That is not the way you learned Christ! For surely you have heard about him and were taught in him, as truth is in Jesus. You were taught to put away your former way of life, your old self, corrupt and deluded by its lusts, and to be renewed in the spirit of your minds, and to clothe yourselves with the new self, created according to the likeness of God in true righteousness and holiness.

Sin and a hard heart once darkened our understanding, alienating from us from the life of God. As we continue to put away our former way of life, being renewed in the spirit of our minds, we grow in the knowledge of the Lord.

We must first believe that we have died to sin and that God has freely given us a new identity of righteousness. Being renewed in the spirit of our minds means that we learn to act and think out of that new identity. To live according to the truth that we are dead to sin and alive to God, is to walk in heaven while on earth.

Romans 12:2 Do not be conformed to this world, but be transformed by the renewing of your minds

As we are transformed by the renewing of our minds, we grow in the knowledge of the Lord and experience the manifest glory of the Lord in greater degrees. It is by first receiving the free gift of righteousness that we are transformed. This *"free gift"* of righteousness is the

Chapter Four—Removing The Veils

knowledge of the Lord made possible through the forgiveness of sins.

Look at these two verses in Romans. The *"free gift"* of righteousness and the *"free gift"* of eternal life are the same thing. Remember that eternal life is to know God,[77] so the *"free gift"* of eternal life is the knowledge of the Lord that comes through Christ. The experiential knowledge of the Lord involves participating in his divine nature, which is righteousness.

Romans 5:17 If, because of the one man's trespass, death exercised dominion through that one, much more surely will those who receive the abundance of grace and the free gift of righteousness exercise dominion in life through the one man, Jesus Christ.

Romans 6:23 For the wages of sin is death, but the free gift of God is eternal life in Christ Jesus our Lord.

If we do sin, we must not withdraw from the Lord's presence. The intent of Satan's accusations is to make us too ashamed to approach God. Yet it is as we draw near to God and look to him that we are transformed. The one thing that we need to do, if we do sin, is to boldly come to the Father!

Hebrews 4:16 Let us therefore approach the throne of grace with boldness, so that we may receive mercy and find grace to help in time of need.

As we saw in Hebrews 9 and 10, to approach the Father is to enter heaven itself. If you sin, the one thing you need to do is to go to heaven now!

---

[77] John 17:3

Approach God now just as when you first came to him—not out of your own righteousness, but because of the free gift of righteousness which you received through Jesus' death and resurrection. Don't draw back in fear! Receive God's mercy and grace in abundance, and let it transform you!

Romans 8:1-2 There is therefore now no condemnation for those who are in Christ Jesus. For the law of the Spirit of life in Christ Jesus has set you free from the law of sin and of death.

I remember hearing the remarkable testimony of a man who was delivered from addiction to pornography. He became a Christian and read in Exodus how Moses talked with God as with a friend.

Exodus 33:9-11 When Moses entered the tent, the pillar of cloud would descend and stand at the entrance of the tent, and the Lord would speak with Moses. When all the people saw the pillar of cloud standing at the entrance of the tent, all the people would rise and bow down, all of them, at the entrance of their tent. Thus the Lord used to speak to Moses face to face, as one speaks to a friend.

When he read this he said *"God, I want to meet you like that!"* He set aside everything to pray and asked God *"God, show me your glory."* Then he met God in a cloud, like Moses did. It was wonderful! He began to do this every day.

This man had so little religious background that when he became a Christian he barely thought anything of his porn habit, because it was so normal to him. It wasn't something that he had really thought of as wrong before. But as he met God, he began to feel uncomfortable about it.

Chapter Four—Removing The Veils

For about 30 days of these encounters he was still looking at porn. He messed up again and again. But every day he came back to meet the Lord. God continued to meet with him, and he loved God's presence! After a month of meeting the Lord like this daily, he stopped looking at porn.

He fell out of sin because he kept going to heaven every day by approaching God, until the presence of the Lord transformed him so much that he no longer had a desire for pornography. He became a partaker in the divine nature, and the free gift of righteousness that he had received bore the fruit of righteousness.[78]

When you approach God and see his beauty and holiness, it can be terrifying! We see a pattern in scripture of people being afraid when they encountered the Lord, but being told not to fear. So don't draw back in fear from the Lord's presence like Adam did. Rather, remind yourself of the blood of Jesus which has washed you and made you clean. Come to the Father boldly and without shame, and let God's presence transform you.

Unforgiveness

When we don't forgive, we won't experience the heavenly reality that Jesus made available to us. We experience heaven to the extent that we participate in God's love and nature. To walk in unforgiveness is to walk in darkness.[79] Bitterness is defiling.[80]

When we don't forgive, we tend to see God through our experiences with other people. Man was created in the image and likeness of God, to reflect his glory. Mankind was meant to be a reflection of what God is like. Yet since all men sinned and fell short of his

---

[78] Hebrews 12:11
[79] 1 John 2:11
[80] Hebrews 12:15

glory, the image that was reflected became distorted. Jesus came as a sinless man so that we could once again see, through a man, what God is like. He said if we see him, we see the Father.[81]

If we don't forgive, we see God through sinful man, the first Adam, the earthly man. Our image of God is distorted. Instead, we must forgive and behold the pure image of God as revealed through Christ, the second Adam, the man of heaven.[82]

Corrie Ten Boom's sister, Betsie, was able to live in heavenly reality while in a concentration camp because she forgave and loved the Nazis who were blinded and full of demons. And Betsie died there. Corrie struggled with forgiveness at times, both when they were in the Ravensbrück camp, and after her release and her sister's death. But God helped her to forgive. Her story is encouraging.

It was at a church service in Munich that I saw him, the former S.S. man who had stood guard at the shower room door in the processing center at Ravensbruck. He was the first of our actual jailers that I had seen since that time. And suddenly it was all there— the roomful of mocking men, the heaps of clothing, Betsie's pain-blanched face.

He came up to me as the church was emptying, beaming and bowing. "How grateful I am for your message, Fraulein." he said. "To think that, as you say, He has washed my sins away!" His hand was thrust out to shake mine.

And I, who had preached so often to the people in Bloemendaal the need to forgive, kept my hand at my side. Even as the angry, vengeful thoughts boiled

---

[81] John 14:9
[82] 1 Corinthians 15:45-47

Chapter Four—Removing The Veils

through me, I saw the sin of them. Jesus Christ had died for this man; was I going to ask for more? Lord Jesus, I prayed, forgive me and help me to forgive him.

I tried to smile; I struggled to raise my hand. I could not. I felt nothing, not the slightest spark of warmth or charity. And so again I breathed a silent prayer. Jesus, I cannot forgive him. Give your forgiveness.

As I took his hand the most incredible thing happened. From my shoulder along my arm and through my hand, a current seemed to pass from me to him, while into my heart sprang a love for this stranger that almost overwhelmed me. And so I discovered that it is not on our forgiveness any more than on our goodness that the world's healing hinges, but on His. When He tells us to love our enemies, He gives, along with the command, the love itself.[83]

Corrie found herself unable to forgive, but asked God to give her his forgiveness. She then entered into a heavenly reality revealed in the gospel, God's forgiveness. She beheld the glory of God that was revealed in Christ. She entered an experiential knowledge of the Lord's glory as Christ's love and forgiveness was expressed through her.

You may think this story sounds supernatural. It is! The whole Christian life is supernatural. In trying times, when we look to the Lord and experience his power, the fact that *"Jesus lives in me"* becomes very real to us. We see that the indwelling Holy Spirit is working in us to will and to do[84] his will.

We forgive by faith. We are empowered to do so when we behold the forgiveness that Jesus showed as he died and said *"Father, forgive them, for they know not*

---

[83] Boom, Corrie Ten; Elizabeth Sherrill; John Sherrill (2006-01-01). The Hiding Place (pp. 247-248). Baker Publishing Group. Kindle Edition.
[84] Philippians 2:13

what they do."[85] Here is something else that Corrie said about forgiveness:

If you have ever seen a country church with a bell in the steeple, you will remember that to get the bell ringing you have to tug awhile. Once it has begun to ring, you merely maintain the momentum. As long as you keep pulling, the bell keeps ringing. Forgiveness is letting go of the rope. It is just that simple. But when you do so, the bell keeps ringing. Momentum is still at work. However, if you keep your hands off the rope, the bell will begin to slow and eventually stop.[86]

Sometimes the bell is still ringing, and you still feel vengeful over what has happened. Then Satan may accuse you, saying *"You haven't really forgiven."* Tell Satan to shut up, then stand firm on the fact that you have forgiven with the forgiveness of Christ, who lives in you.

Until we forgive, we will be overcome by evil instead of overcoming it.[87] But if you have turned to the Lord you are an overcomer, because whatever is born of God overcomes the world![88] Just as God is love, you are love and you will find that even when it seems impossible, you continue to love, because Jesus lives in you.

Richard Wurmbrand left Romania after enduring fourteen years of unspeakable tortures in communist prisons. His last act before leaving was to leave a flower on the grave of the colonel who had ordered his arrest and his years of torture.

---

[85] Luke 23:34
[86] http://spiritfilledchristianliving.com/my-favorite-christian-quotes-about-forgiveness/
[87] Romans 12:21
[88] 1 John 5:4

Chapter Four—Removing The Veils

Wurmbrand said he hated Communism, but loved Communists with all his heart. Communists could kill Christians but could never kill their love, not even their love for their murderers. He didn't have the slightest bitterness or resentment towards his torturers.[89]

His perspective was the perspective of a heavenly person. Even the greatest of evils could not make him bitter or keep him from constantly beholding the glory of God in the face of Christ.

He also described the love and forgiveness shown by many other Christians who suffered horrendous things. Christians who were tortured, whipped, forced to swallow spoons full of salt, deprived of food, water, and clothing, with fifty pounds of chains on their feet, prayed fervently for the communists!

Wurmbrand stated that just as Daniel's three friends didn't smell like smoke when God delivered them from the fiery furnace, Christians who had been in Communist prisons didn't smell like bitterness against the Communists.[90]

It's interesting that Wurmbrand also said Christians knew Christ's love toward the communists by their own love for them. We behold God's glory as the Holy Spirit in us loves people in a way that's not naturally possible. Sometimes we know how great God's love is when the Holy Spirit manifests it through us.

Dan Mohler once said, *"Just as when you squeeze an orange, orange juice comes out, when you squeeze a Christian, Christ should come out."* When

---

[89] Wurmbrand, Richard (2010-09-30). Tortured for Christ (Kindle Locations 948-955). Living Sacrifice Book Company. Kindle Edition.

[90] Wurmbrand, Richard (2010-09-30). Tortured for Christ (Kindle Locations 1157-1159). Living Sacrifice Book Company. Kindle Edition.

these Christians in Eastern Europe were squeezed and pressed, the love of God flowed out of them all the more. They were heavenly people.

Emotional Numbness

Sometimes we experience such pain or betrayal that it seems our hearts close up and we stop loving. It feels like it hurts too much to love, and so we become numb. In my experience this is not the same as unforgiveness.

There have been times when I know I was not bitter towards anyone, and I continued to love people with all my heart, but I felt great emotional pain. My heart began to close to being able to express that love.

In her book *"The Hiding Place,"* Corrie Ten Boom shared the story of her romance with a young man she called *"Karel,"* and its painful ending. She and Karel were deeply in love, yet he married another due to strong family and cultural expectations that he marry within his *"class"* and economic status. I have identified with Corrie's emotional pain on several occasions. Listen to the wise advice of her father, Caspar, when she was heartbroken:

Somehow the half-hour passed. Somehow I managed to shake her hand, then Karel's hand, and to wish them every happiness. Betsie took them down to the door.

Before it clicked shut, I was fleeing up the stairs to my own room at the top of the house where the tears could come. How long I lay on my bed sobbing for the one love of my life I do not know.

Later, I heard Father's footsteps coming up the stairs. For a moment I was a little girl again, waiting for him to tuck the blankets tight. But this was a hurt that no blanket could shut out, and suddenly I was afraid of what Father would say. Afraid he would say, "There'll be someone else soon," and that forever afterward this

Chapter Four—Removing The Veils

untruth would lie between us. For in some deep part of me I knew already that there would not— soon or ever— be anyone else.

The sweet cigar-smell came into the room with Father. And of course he did not say the false, idle words. "Corrie," he began instead, "do you know what hurts so very much? It's love. Love is the strongest force in the world, and when it is blocked that means pain. "There are two things we can do when this happens. We can kill the love so that it stops hurting. But then of course part of us dies, too. Or, Corrie, we can ask God to open up another route for that love to travel.

"God loves Karel— even more than you do— and if you ask Him, He will give you His love for this man, a love nothing can prevent, nothing destroy. Whenever we cannot love in the old, human way, Corrie, God can give us the perfect way."

I did not know, as I listened to Father's footsteps winding back down the stairs, that he had given me more than the key to this hard moment. I did not know that he had put into my hands the secret that would open far darker rooms than this— places where there was not, on a human level, anything to love at all.[91]

It hurts when love is rejected. This is true not only of romantic relationships. When you work to help people, preach the gospel to them, or tell them what Jesus has done for you, some reject your love. They may not understand you or trust your intentions. When you pour your life into helping people on the path towards recovery from addiction, and they relapse, it hurts. When you take a homeless couple with their baby into your

---

[91] Boom, Corrie Ten; Elizabeth Sherrill; John Sherrill (2006-01-01). The Hiding Place (p. 60). Baker Publishing Group. Kindle Edition.

home (as I once did), and the husband steals and destroys things in your house, it hurts.

When you go as an aid worker to starving and homeless multitudes of people who have suffered a terrible natural disaster, you face a need that feels overwhelming. It would be much easier to stay home and hide from it. Sometimes we face such pain that we are tempted to close our hearts and become numb, because it hurts too much to love.

We may close our hearts when we become afraid that loving and responding to love will only cause more pain. If so, we become numb. This numbness dims our awareness of our Heavenly Father's love. It hinders us from fully knowing and living in the heavenly reality of unspeakable joy in God's presence.

When your love is rejected, refuse to fall to self-pity. Keep loving. Ask God to help you keep your heart open. Ask God to give you ways to express his perfect love. Jesus never stopped loving and never closed his heart, no matter how much it hurt.

Caspar Ten Boom was right that love is the strongest force in the world. Nothing can separate you from the love of God, and if you choose to love, nothing can make you stop loving. The cross did not stop Jesus from loving and saying *"Father, forgive them, for they know not what they do."* The tortures of the Communists tormentors could not stop the love of the Christians in the Soviet Union.

If nothing can stop you from loving, nothing can stop you from possessing heavenly joy. The joy that is in heaven springs from the love of God. When your joy no longer comes from your circumstances but from God's love flowing through your heart, you have a joy that can never be taken from you. When God's love flows through you, you always have something to give. You are immeasurably rich because that supply will never run

Chapter Four—Removing The Veils

out and the flow of it will continue to increase as you grow in the knowledge of the Lord.

Jesus said that *"It is more blessed to give than to receive."*[92] It is blessed to receive, but being able to give is the greater blessing. People can take all you have, but they can never take away the greater blessing of being able to give, because nothing can stop you from giving when you have an endless supply of God's love and his Holy Spirit flowing through you. That flow will continue to increase as you grow in the knowledge of the Lord.

When I feel numb, I ask the Lord to help me have an open heart and to not stop loving. Sometimes love is rejected, whether it is romantic love, or whether it is reaching out to people with God's love. I have felt the pain of rejected love. Like Mr. Ten Boom advised, I ask God to show me another route for that love to travel.

Love is unstoppable. If you feel numb with emotional pain, go to heaven now. Approach the Father and let the rivers of his love flow into you. As you receive God's love, you will be empowered to keep loving.

Corrie also shared about seeing her mother after a stroke. Her mother could no longer feed the hungry and clothe the poor as she had previously. Although the stroke was somewhat confining, Corrie's mother was free, because her heart was full of love! This helped Corrie later on to experience the freedom God's love imparts. The remembrance of this truth sustained her even while she was imprisoned. Nothing can lock up love or confine it. Love sets our spirits free, and that freedom is a heavenly reality to which we have constant access.

---

[92] Acts 20:35

"Mama's love had always been the kind that acted itself out with soup pot and sewing basket. But now that these things were taken away, the love seemed as whole as before.

She sat in her chair at the window and loved us. She loved the people she saw in the street—and beyond: her love took in the city, the land of Holland, the world. And so I learned that love is larger than the walls that shut it in"[93]

Lies Which Exalt Themselves Against The Knowledge Of God

Any belief that undermines the truth and implications of the gospel will keep us from seeing God accurately. Such lies hinder us from experiencing heaven now. The good news is that these hindering beliefs can be easily dealt with. We can see the Lord as never before and experience heaven now. Our mouths can be filled with God's praise at all times, and our faces can be radiant!

For many years I never saw a person healed through my own hands, although I myself had been healed by God. I thought it was usually God's will to heal people but that there were some exceptions. This was because I had a poor theology about Job and about Paul's *"thorn in the flesh."* My theology was incompatible with scripture's teaching about healing in Christ's atonement and in salvation. These lies clouded my view of God's nature and his will.

As soon as these *"arguments,"* which exalted themselves against the knowledge of God, were torn down in my thinking, people began to be healed when I laid my hands on them. It felt as if heaven had opened,

---

[93] Boom, Corrie Ten; Elizabeth Sherrill; John Sherrill (2006-01-01). The Hiding Place (p. 64). Baker Publishing Group. Kindle Edition.

Chapter Four—Removing The Veils

but in reality, heaven had been open the whole time. As *"veils"* of lies were removed, I started to see the Lord as he really is and I experienced the heavenly reality of God's presence more than I ever had before. I grew in an experiential, participatory knowledge of the Lord and of his goodness.

In the next chapter I share a vision in which God showed me some hindering mindsets that are common among Christians. They are mental constructs which deny Jesus' coming in the flesh, his sacrifice for sins, and his resurrection.

The second book in this series deals with fear—a form of misdirected worship, or idolatry. The third book explores in greater detail the lies of the antichrist spirit, which denies that Jesus came in the flesh. All of these things are *"veils"* which can hinder us from seeing the Lord as he truly is.

As I have grown in knowing the Lord and in recognizing these lies for what they were, tearing down the *"arguments"* in my mind which exalted themselves against the knowledge of the Lord, the manifestation of heaven's reality increased in my experience and in demonstration through my life.

I'm sharing the stories of what happened when I recognized these lies. I pray they would encourage you to also come into a heavenly experience and a greater knowledge of the Lord than you ever have before.

If you apply these simple gospel truths, they will bring you into a present experience and demonstration of heaven. If you are not experiencing heaven now, you can be sure there are *"arguments"* that need to be dismantled and *"veils"* that must be removed.

5. The Vision
Why Do I Feel Frustrated?
There was a period of time when I did an in-depth study of prayer and spent many hours praying, yet I felt frustrated with the results. I had never laid my hands on anybody and seen them healed. Yet I believed in miracles, because the Bible taught about them, and I myself had been healed.

Then at the *"Healing Fusion"* conference, I became convinced it is always God's will to heal people, as much as it is to forgive their sins. That was when the miracles began. God showed me that he had always wanted to do these miracles in my life, but there were some things I needed to understand.

I had a vision four years later, highlighting beliefs which had hindered me from experiencing God's power in my life. I realized I had unintentionally denied some fundamental gospel truths for many years. No wonder I had been so frustrated!

Similarly, I realized that many other people were continuing to unknowingly deny the gospel. This was why they were not presently experiencing heaven's reality, made possible by believing gospel truth. It was why they felt spiritually poor. I saw the need to hold fast to the truth of the gospel and tear down these *"proud arguments"* that are raised against the knowledge of the Lord.

The vision I received was not seen with physical eyes, but came as a clear picture in my mind. It highlighted important scriptural truths to help believers pray effectively.

Toronto

I had this experience while visiting some good friends who lead a small church in Toronto, Canada. They had asked me to share with the congregation. Some days before I arrived, I came down with a cold and sore throat. I was going to speak on healing and miracles, but I was sick! However, I knew it was God's will that I be healed, and that whatever I felt physically did not change the reality of his word.

I decided to stand firm, knowing the Lord wanted to bless these people in Toronto. I was confident that no matter how I felt, people would be healed if I laid hands on them. By the time I arrived in Toronto, I had just recovered from the cold. I was no longer sick, but my throat still felt dry and scratchy.

On Sunday morning I still wasn't sure exactly what to speak, so I sat down for a while with my Bible to pray and to ask God for the message that would benefit the congregation. That was when I saw this picture.

Banging On The Wall Of Heaven

In the vision I saw a big wall. Many people were praying and fasting, and banging with their fists on this wall. They were crying out *"Oh God, that you would rend the heavens and come down!"*[94] They were working very hard, endlessly begging and pleading for God to open the heavens and send revival. They were asking God to come to them with a mighty visitation, and they were seeking authority over the works of the enemy.

---

[94] Isaiah 64:1

Chapter Five—The Vision

Some of them had a big tree trunk that they were using as a battering ram, and they were trying to break through the wall. They were frustrated because it didn't seem to be working.

Yet right beside these people was an open door in the wall. They were trying to break through the wall, but seemed blind to the door which they could simply walk through. There were only a few people who saw the door, and they walked in easily. They were full of joy and their faces were radiant. Miracles were happening all around them.

They were also praying unceasingly. However, their prayers were answered quickly, before they could even close their mouths from forming the words. The reason they were constantly praying was because they knew they had what they asked of the Father.

They were continually asking and receiving from the Father, and exercising dominion over sickness and the works of the enemy. They had a fullness of joy that was evident as they asked and received.

1 John 5:14-15 And this is the boldness we have in him, that if we ask anything according to his will, he hears us. And if we know that he hears us in whatever we ask, we know that we have obtained the requests made of him.

Isaiah 65:24 Before they call I will answer, while they are yet speaking I will hear.

John 16:24 (NKJV) Until now you have asked nothing in My name. Ask, and you will receive, that your joy may be full.

The Interpretation

I understood that the place the people were trying to enter was the true Most Holy place which Hebrews 9 and 10 talks about. As we saw in chapter one, this Holiest Place is heaven itself.[95] The door is the body of Christ which was torn for us so that we could come to the Father. It corresponds to the veil which covered the Holiest Place, which Hebrews teaches was Jesus' body.[96]

The first group was frustrated because they were trying to enter God's presence through prayer rather than through Christ. They were never going to get through the wall that way, because the only way it is possible to enter the Holiest Place is through the curtain that was torn, Jesus body.

I saw that in their approach to prayer, they were denying that Jesus came in the flesh, denying that a sacrifice for sin had been made, and denying the resurrection from the dead. They didn't realize what they were saying; nor did they comprehend the reason everything was difficult and ineffective.

The few who entered through the door were living in heaven while on earth. They didn't pray in order to get into the Holiest Place. They prayed because they were already in God's presence, in heaven, and had entered through Christ.

As a teenager, I had often been in the first category of intercessors. I knew what it was like to pound on a wall day and night, asking God to open the heavens and send revival. I remember the frustration. I read many stories of miracles and revival in other times and places, but wondered why I didn't experience the same in my life. I remember thinking I needed to use the battering ram of prayer until I could get breakthrough and experience revival, yet the breakthrough never came.

In the vision, the second group of believers demonstrated what I had come to experience in the last

---

[95] Hebrews 9:24
[96] Hebrews 10:20

Chapter Five—The Vision

few years. It became natural to pray all the time, because prayers were being answered all the time. Prayers were answered before I prayed them. I would just think a thought, and miracles would happen. It was glorious! I was already in heaven, and it was so much easier than before.

Oh, That You Would Rend The Heavens And Come Down!

This was one of the prayers that the people in the first group kept repeating. Although this is a scriptural prayer, it's a prayer that was fulfilled in Christ's coming and by his sacrifice. Therefore, to continue to pray it is to act and think as if we still need a savior to die for us. It is denying the gospel without our realizing what we are saying.

Isaiah 64.1 (NIV) Oh, that you would rend the heavens and come down, that the mountains would tremble before you!

I didn't know this prayer in Isaiah had already been fulfilled until I understand Hebrews 9 and 10. Jesus' body is the veil that was rent. The true Holy of Holies which this veil covered is heaven itself. Therefore, the heavens were rent when Jesus' body was torn on the cross.

The action of *"rending the heavens"* corresponds to Jesus' atonement. To ask God to rend the heavens is like asking God to provide a sacrifice for sin and a way into his presence, a way of salvation. He already did!

In the same way, when Jesus' came in the flesh, as a man, God came down! He became one of us, accessible to us, so that we could approach him face to face, as to a man. This was what Job longed for![97] To keep begging God to come down is to act as if Jesus never came in the flesh. God came down, and he is Immanuel, God with us,[98] who will never leave us.[99] He promised to be with us always.[100]

Yet I had spent many years praying this prayer of Isaiah and singing in worship songs *"God, rend the heavens and come down!"* The logical conclusion of my prayer is that I was asking God to provide a sacrifice for sins so I could have access to his presence.

That which I prayed without understanding was in total denial of the gospel message of what Christ *had already done* for me! I was asking God to rend the heavens, as if Jesus' body never was torn for me! I was also begging God to come down, as if Jesus had never come in the flesh!

Of course I didn't realize this at the time. In hindsight, I saw that years of powerlessness and frustration were caused by my acknowledging the gospel but denying it at the same time! In other words, I was double minded! I acknowledged that Jesus' body was torn so I could approach God, but then begged God to rend the heavens. I acknowledged that Jesus came in the flesh, but then begged God to come down.

James 1:6-8 (NIV) But when you ask, you must believe and not doubt, because the one who doubts is like a wave of the sea, blown and tossed by the wind. That person should not expect to receive anything from the Lord. Such a person is double-minded and unstable in all they do.

---

[97] Job 9:32-35
[98] Isaiah 7:14
[99] Hebrews 13:5
[100] Matthew 28:20

Chapter Five—The Vision

I was frustrated because I was double minded. The fact that I was praying these prayers showed that I still did not fully understand the gospel or the implications thereof.

Since the gospel is the power of God unto salvation,[101] if we are really believing it we should be continuously experiencing the power of God bringing salvation. That salvation should be evident in the power, love, and unspeakable joy that exude from our lives. If that is not the case, we should ask, *"Am I really believing the gospel?"*

I had thought I believed the gospel, but in my prayers, mindset, and actions, I denied Jesus came in the flesh, I denied Christ's sacrifice for sins which gave me access to God's presence, and I denied that Christ rose from the dead. The reason I often felt the gospel wasn't working for me was because I was thinking and acting as if it weren't true!

Trying To Bring Christ Down From Heaven Or To Bring Him Up From The Dead

The Holy Spirit highlighted this well-known passage to me from Romans chapter 10. I had always seen the application of Romans chapter 10 in the light of salvation past, or being born again. However, I now saw how it relates to salvation present. As we embrace the truth of the gospel, we can walk right now in the heavenly reality of God's presence.

Romans 10:6-9 But the righteousness that comes from faith says, "Do not say in your heart, 'Who will ascend into heaven?'" (that is, to bring Christ down) "or 'Who will descend into the abyss?'" (that is, to bring Christ up from the dead). But what does it say?

---

[101] Romans 1:16

"The word is near you, on your lips and in your heart"(that is, the word of faith that we proclaim); because if you confess with your lips that Jesus is Lord and believe in your heart that God raised him from the dead, you will be saved.

When I was a part of that group who were pounding on the wall instead of entering through the Door, I was trying to bring Christ down by ascending into heaven, or to bring Christ up from the dead by descending into the abyss. What does this imply?

Ascending Into Heaven Or Descending Into The Abyss

If you believe the gospel, you have already ascended into heaven! The gospel teaches that we were raised with Christ and seated with him in heavenly places:

Ephesians 1:18-22 (NIV) I pray that the eyes of your heart may be enlightened in order that you may know the hope to which he has called you, the riches of his glorious inheritance in his holy people, and his incomparably great power for us who believe. That power is the same as the mighty strength he exerted when he raised Christ from the dead and seated him at his right hand in the heavenly realms, far above all rule and authority, power and dominion, and every name that is invoked, not only in the present age but also in the one to come. And God placed all things under his feet and appointed him to be head over everything for the church, which is his body, the fullness of him who fills everything in every way.

Ephesians 2:6 (NIV) God raised us up with Christ and seated us with him in the heavenly realms in Christ Jesus

Chapter Five—The Vision

Do you see what the resurrection of the dead means for us? It gives us authority and dominion. Jesus was seated far above all rule, authority, power, dominion, and given a name above every other name. When we were raised with Jesus in newness of life, we were seated with him, far above all rule, authority, power, dominion, and every name that can be invoked. It is a fact. It has been accomplished through Christ's resurrection.

Luke 10:19 (NIV) I have given you authority to trample on snakes and scorpions and to overcome all the power of the enemy; nothing will harm you.

Matthew 10:1 (NIV) Jesus called his twelve disciples to him and gave them authority to drive out impure spirits and to heal every disease and sickness.

All the time I spent banging against a wall, I was trying to attain to a level of authority where I could cast out demons and heal the sick. I was trying to attain a higher level of spirituality, when according to scripture I had already been raised with Christ to the highest level possible. In Christ, there are no *"levels"* of authority. There is only *"all authority."* There is, however, a maturing in the knowledge of Christ with an increasing confidence and boldness in the Lord.

By trying to *"ascend into heaven,"* I acted as if Jesus' resurrection had no application for me. I mentally acknowledged that Jesus rose from the dead, and that I was raised with him. Yet my prayers revealed that my beliefs did not embrace the provisions of Christ's resurrection. I was double minded because I confessed Jesus rose from the dead, while denying what his resurrection had accomplished. My faith in the message of the gospel had been undermined.

Present Access To Heaven

The book of Romans says that to attempt to ascend into heaven is to try to bring Christ down. In my prayers, as I was banging against that wall, I was trying to bring God down. I was fasting and praying, begging him to come and bring revival. I was frustrated because it seemed he never came; as if I always needed to fast and pray more, until I could reach the tipping point with my prayers and get him to come.

I didn't realize I was denying that Jesus came in the flesh by continually begging God to come. I was double-minded in that I mentally acknowledged Jesus came in the flesh, but I prayed as if he never did.

Because of my double mindedness, I did not apprehend the fullness of Christ's blessing; the power, dominion, and joy that are the fruit of believing the gospel. The gospel is meant to bring us into a present reality of heaven on earth. Our faces should be glowing, our hearts overflowing, so it becomes evident to all that as Jesus is, so are we in this world.[102]

We are also descending into the abyss (trying to bring Christ up from the dead) when we try to attain authority over evil. We don't need to try to bring Christ up from the dead! He has already risen!

In my prayers, I descended into the abyss as I focused on the evil I was trying to overcome, and my heart became heavy. Instead of beholding the glory of God in the face of Christ, the evil in the world which I confronted filled my vision. I felt heavy.

My prayers made it evident that I did not believe Christ had already risen from the dead and had overcome this evil. I denied Christ's resurrection by trying to attain victory over that which Christ had conquered. Because I doubted the gospel, the power and authority of the gospel wasn't evident through my life.

---

[102] 1 John 4:17

Chapter Five—The Vision

I was still born again. I was still a child of God. My name was written in the book of life. But I was experiencing very little of the present heavenly reality that salvation brings. If we are experiencing anything less than heaven on earth, we should consider how much our mindsets and belief systems are in line with gospel truths.

We can get so used to mentally acknowledging the teachings of the gospel but denying the implications of those truths, that our hearts become numb to the gospel message. Then we can't perceive the greatness of its glory. It seems too good to be true, but it really is true!

The Dangers Of Descending Into The Abyss

In my futile attempts to bring Christ up from the dead, I acted as if he had never resurrected; as if he had not already been victorious.

This can be dangerous. People often get hurt when they take this approach to spiritual warfare. They are challenging evil from a place of deception, not from the position of believing the gospel and of resurrection power.

For example, there have been instances of a person *"interceding"* for someone who had a sickness, then getting the same sickness or disease and thinking they are *"carrying"* the sickness in intercession for that person. I've read books promoting this teaching and I have met people who claimed that they were carrying someone else's sickness.

First of all, it isn't hard to get someone healed! It doesn't take hours of anguish in prayer! It simply takes a command with faith in Jesus' name. Secondly, this is a denial of the gospel. You shouldn't be carrying anyone else's sicknesses any more than you should be trying to carry their sins. Jesus already carried them.

On one occasion, I ministered healing to a group of people adhering to New Age beliefs. They understood many things about the spiritual realm, but they didn't understand the way of salvation that Jesus made for us. After many were healed, a kind lady gave me some advice.

She said *"You are a very good person, and you have been taking sicknesses off of so many people. But now, listen to me. Take the branch of this tree and transfer the sicknesses into the tree. If you do not, you can get very sick by continuing to carry the sicknesses that you took out of all these people."*

My heart was broken. I explained to her that I wasn't carrying these people's sicknesses, but that Jesus already did. Jesus carried our sicknesses and sins so that we would not have to. She understood the spiritual principle of transference, but she was totally missing the gospel!

These New Agers understood many spiritual principles, but they were blind to the salvation that can only come through Christ. A Christian who believes he is carrying someone else's disease is doing the same thing that a shaman or spiritist healer does.

Such people do not confront the disease from the place of faith in Christ's resurrection and victory. They try to overcome it as if Jesus had not already done so, so they become vulnerable to the afflicting spirit they confront. A deceiving spirit tells them that they are carrying this sickness in intercession for the other person. In doing so, the deceiving spirit denies the atonement of Christ.

I know this may sound wild to some readers, but we have learned from experience that many sicknesses and pains are caused by an afflicting spirit which must be expelled.

On one occasion, a group of young people surrounded a porn convention and decided to *"pull down"* the principality of lust that was there. All of them soon became addicted to porn.

The fact that they tried to *"pull down"* this principality showed they did not confront it from a place of gospel power. They didn't act as people who were raised and seated with Christ in heavenly places, *"far above all rule and authority, power and dominion, and every name that is named."* If they had believed this, they would not try to *"pull down"* a principality, but would simply trample it under their feet by preaching and demonstrating the gospel.

Luke 10:17-20 The seventy returned with joy, saying, "Lord, in your name even the demons submit to us!" He said to them, "I watched Satan fall from heaven like a flash of lightning. See, I have given you authority to tread on snakes and scorpions, and over all the power of the enemy; and nothing will hurt you. Nevertheless, do not rejoice at this, that the spirits submit to you, but rejoice that your names are written in heaven."

Jesus' disciples had returned from healing the sick, casting out demons, and proclaiming that the kingdom of heaven was at hand. At their return Jesus said *"I saw Satan fall like lightening from heaven."* Jesus gave them authority, and then they trampled on the power of the enemy. In the same way, we should not be trying to obtain authority over evil. Instead, we are to simply trample upon it. Evil was defeated and we gained authority and a place *"far above"* all evil, with the resurrection of Christ.

I know others who, many years ago, got together and decided to *"pull down"* a *"Leviathan spirit."* For a few years, every horrible thing imaginable seemed to happen to them. Their problem was that they were *"descending into the abyss"* instead of understanding that they were seated with Christ in heavenly places.

By failing to understand the power and authority of Christ's resurrection, it was as if they were trying to *"bring Christ up from the dead."* Instead of trying to *"pull down"* the *"Leviathan spirit,"* they should have focused on trampling over the enemy by demonstrating God's kingdom with power.

We do this by acting on what Jesus taught us- preaching the gospel, healing the sick, cleansing the lepers, and casting out demons.[103] We trample over Satan's power as we overcome evil with good.[104]

In reaction to many people's painful experiences from *"descending into the abyss"* in *"spiritual warfare,"* a doctrine arose, based on a dream, that we only have authority over some of the power of the enemy. It said that we can only exercise authority over small demons that afflict individuals, but we can only ask God to deal with principalities.

However, this doctrine is confusing, wholly unbiblical, and very poorly argued. Jesus said that he gave us authority to trample on all the power of the enemy, and nothing would hurt us.[105] Ephesians chapters one and two are clear that we are seated far above all the power of our enemy. We are united to the Lord as the body of Christ and have the same authority over evil as Jesus does.

The real problem was that people tried to confront evil in such a way that they were acting as if Christ did not rise from the dead. The real need was to understand the power of Christ's resurrection, and of our resurrection with him.

---

[103] Matthew 10:8
[104] Romans 12:21
[105] Luke 10:19

Chapter Five—The Vision

Anyone who believes that we have authority over only some of the power of the enemy should consider the fruit of Carlos Annacondia's ministry in the Argentine revival. Annacondia addressed Satan directly, saying *"Listen to me Satan! You're going to let these people go."*

Large percentages of the population in big cities came to Christ, with many thousands of people delivered from demons. People who tried to kill Annacondia fell to the ground. In one city, Mar del Plata, eighty-three thousand people accepted Christ — 20 percent of the population.[106] His book, *"Listen to me, Satan"*[107] is well worth reading.

The Word Is Near You

The righteousness that comes from faith does not try to ascend into heaven, or descend into the abyss. Rather, it says *"the word is near you."* If you confess with your mouth that Jesus is Lord, and believe in your heart that God has raised him from the dead, you will be saved.

We have heard this promise applied to being born again— salvation past— and it is true. But we have seen that a scriptural view of salvation includes not only forgiveness, but healing, deliverance, peace, and the fullness of the heavenly reality created by God's presence. Therefore, we can also apply the promise of Romans 10 to God's present deliverance in our lives and around us.

Stop trying to ascend into heaven or to descend into the abyss. Stop trying to attain to the victory which has already been accomplished. Stop trying to reach up

---

[106] Listen to Me, Satan Page 145
[107] Annacondia, Carlos, 1998: Listen To Me, Satan: Creation House Publishers

into heaven as if God were far off. He is here. The word is near you. You have the gospel, and in it is your victory.

Stop denying the sacrifice of Christ by begging God to rend the heavens. Whatever you face, confess with your mouth that Jesus is Lord over it. Believe in your heart that God has raised Christ from the dead, and raised you up with him— to be seated with him far above all rule, authority, power, dominion, and every name that is named.

The Fruit Of This Teaching

I preached what I saw in the vision that Sunday. I also shared many testimonies of healing miracles. I was coughing a lot. Even though I was over the cold, my throat was itchy and it felt like something was stuck in it. I was talking about healing, but for a while it was difficult to speak because I kept coughing.

The pastor looked worried, but I kept going with a smile. I had driven all the way to Toronto to speak to these people, and I was determined not to let anything keep me from sharing with them. I was here to see God glorified, and miracles were going to happen.

Then suddenly, my throat cleared up and I was better. When I finished, I asked everyone who needed to be healed to raise their hands. I estimated it was about two-thirds of the people. I tried to get them to lay hands on each other, but I couldn't convince them to minister to each other. They wanted me to pray for them.

I prayed for them and watched them being healed one after another. One lady had throat cancer, and she felt God's fire touch her throat. I stood there, weeping, overwhelmed by the feeling that Jesus himself was standing there beside me. And I remembered his words:

Matthew 28:20 I am with you always, to the end of the age.

Chapter Five—The Vision

To the best of my knowledge, everyone except for one person who was there and asked for healing ministry was healed. One lady wore glasses, but when we left, she still needed her glasses. All of the others had pain leave, and could do what they could not do before. If it was not an immediately testable condition, they felt heat or power in their bodies.

We know it was also God's will to heal the lady who wore glasses. We don't look at what is seen, but at what is unseen, for what is seen is temporary, but what is unseen is eternal.[108] So I look into the eternal realm in which that woman is already healed. The eye condition is temporary. That means it also is about to end.

When the message of the gospel is understood, the power of God will always be evident.

---

[108] 2 Corinthians 4:8

6. Dead To The Earthly Man, Resurrected As A Man Of Heaven

The First Adam And The Second Adam

The Bible teaches that Adam was the *"earthly man"* but Jesus was the second Adam and was the *"man of heaven."* Part of what is accomplished in salvation is that just as Christ died, we die to the earthly man. As Christ was raised from the dead, we are raised from death as heavenly people.

1 Corinthians 15:45-49 Thus it is written, "The first man, Adam, became a living being;" the last Adam became a life-giving spirit. But it is not the spiritual that is first, but the physical, and then the spiritual. The first man was from the earth, a man of dust; the second man is from heaven. As was the man of dust, so are those who are of the dust; and as is the man of heaven, so are those who are of heaven. Just as we have borne the image of the man of dust, we will also bear the image of the man of heaven.

The last verse says that we will bear the image of the man of heaven. This is future, and is speaking of the bodily resurrection. However, even though we have not yet been resurrected bodily, scripture teaches that our spirits have been resurrected with Christ in newness of life.

Present Access To Heaven

Romans 6:3-4 Do you not know that all of us who have been baptized into Christ Jesus were baptized into his death? Therefore we have been buried with him by baptism into death, so that, just as Christ was raised from the dead by the glory of the Father, so we too might walk in newness of life.

Ephesians 2:4-7 But God, who is rich in mercy, out of the great love with which he loved us even when we were dead through our trespasses, made us alive together with Christ— by grace you have been saved— and raised us up with him and seated us with him in the heavenly places in Christ Jesus, so that in the ages to come he might show the immeasurable riches of his grace in kindness toward us in Christ Jesus.

This is why the previous verse in 1 Corinthians 15 says *"as is the man of heaven, so are those who are of heaven."* This is present tense because it is present reality. Jesus is the man of heaven, and those who are born again have also been raised as heavenly people. When you are baptized you go under the water as an earthly man. You come out as a man of heaven, a new creation.

Colossians 2:12 ...when you were buried with him in baptism, you were also raised with him through faith in the power of God, who raised him from the dead.

2 Corinthians 5:17 So if anyone is in Christ, there is a new creation: everything old has passed away; see, everything has become new!

1 Peter 1:3 By his great mercy he has given us a new birth into a living hope through the resurrection of Jesus Christ from the dead

Chapter Six—Dead To The Earthly Man, Resurrected As A Man Of Heaven

Just as Jesus is the man of heaven, you also are now a man (or woman) of heaven. This is your new identity. It was accomplished by faith in Jesus' death and resurrection. Scripture teaches us to take this as a fact, and so to put off the earthly man, and put on the heavenly man.

1 John 4:17...as he is, so are we in this world.

Ephesians 4:24 ...clothe yourselves with the new self, created according to the likeness of God in true righteousness and holiness.

We are no longer to act or to think like mere men. Since we are heavenly people, our minds are to be set on heavenly things and not earthly things. We must become so aware of the reality in God's presence that our attention is always captured by it.

Our lives are hidden in Christ. And where is Christ? He is seated at the right hand of God in heavenly places. We are on earth, but we are in heaven at the same time. Heaven is also in us, because the true holy of holies, heaven itself, is within us. Our bodies are temples of the Holy Spirit.[109]

Colossians 3:1-3 So if you have been raised with Christ, seek the things that are above, where Christ is, seated at the right hand of God. Set your minds on things that are above, not on things that are on earth, for you have died, and your life is hidden with Christ in God.

---

[109] 1 Corinthians 6:19

Similarly, Jesus, the *"man of heaven"* was on earth and in heaven at the same time. Let's look at what John 3 says in the NKJV:

John 3:12-13 (NKJV) If I have told you earthly things and you do not believe, how will you believe if I tell you heavenly things? No one has ascended to heaven but He who came down from heaven, that is, the Son of Man who is in heaven.

Wow, what a statement! Jesus spoke of himself being in heaven at the same time that he was on earth. When Jesus said that none but he had ascended to heaven, he was speaking before his death, burial and resurrection. The way into the true Holiest Place, heaven itself, had not yet been opened to all who believe.

But now, through the body of Christ that was torn, the way has been made for us to enter the Holiest Place. Therefore, like Jesus, we can be in heaven while on earth. As Ephesians teaches, we have ascended to heaven, because we were raised with Christ and are seated with him in heavenly places. We can say along with Jesus *"I am in heaven,"* even as we walk on earth.

Jesus told Nicodemus that he didn't understand even when he spoke of earthly things. Yet Jesus wanted him to understand heavenly things! Since we are heavenly people, we should understand heavenly things. We have been given the mind of Christ,[110] who is the man of heaven. The spirit of Christ that is within us thinks according to God's wisdom and according to heavenly realities. God wants us to be transformed by the renewing of our minds. Then we will think in accordance with the spirit of Christ that is within us.

---

[110] 1 Corinthians 2:16

Chapter Six—Dead To The Earthly Man, Resurrected As A Man Of Heaven

If you are born again, you are a man of heaven, so you should be heavenly-minded. Wherever you go, you should be aware of heavenly realities. These are the eternal realities which cannot be seen with earthly eyes, but which we know by the spirit of Christ that lives in us. Earthly wisdom is foolishness to God. Heavenly wisdom looks like foolishness to those who are earthly-minded.

2 Corinthians 4:18 ...we look not at what can be seen but at what cannot be seen; for what can be seen is temporary, but what cannot be seen is eternal.

1 Corinthians 1:20-25 Where is the one who is wise? Where is the scribe? Where is the debater of this age? Has not God made foolish the wisdom of the world? For since, in the wisdom of God, the world did not know God through wisdom, God decided, through the foolishness of our proclamation, to save those who believe.

For Jews demand signs and Greeks desire wisdom, but we proclaim Christ crucified, a stumbling block to Jews and foolishness to Gentiles, but to those who are the called, both Jews and Greeks, Christ the power of God and the wisdom of God. For God's foolishness is wiser than human wisdom, and God's weakness is stronger than human strength.

If you think according to heavenly wisdom, you will seem foolish to many people. You will appear foolish, but God will use you to shame the wise and the strong. You will look like nothing, but will bring to nothing the things that are. As we gaze into the eternal heavenly reality of God's presence, we subjugate temporary, earthly realities of sin and death around us.

1 Corinthians 1:26-31 Consider your own call, brothers and sisters: not many of you were wise by human standards, not many were powerful, not many were of noble birth. But God chose what is foolish in the world to shame the wise; God chose what is weak in the world to shame the strong; God chose what is low and despised in the world, things that are not, to reduce to nothing things that are, so that no one might boast in the presence of God.

He is the source of your life in Christ Jesus, who became for us wisdom from God, and righteousness and sanctification and redemption, in order that, as it is written, "Let the one who boasts, boast in the Lord."

We are to think and speak of heavenly things; as ones who are above all earthly things. Jesus, the man of heaven, said he was above all. Now we also are seated with him in heavenly places, far above all rule and authority, power and dominion, and every name that is named.

We will see the heavenly reality trump the temporary earthly reality around us, as we declare, "Kingdom of God, come! Will of God, be done, on earth as it is in heaven!" The eternal heavenly order is more real than any temporary, earthly condition.

John 3:31 The one who comes from above is above all; the one who is of the earth belongs to the earth and speaks about earthly things. The one who comes from heaven is above all.

Matthew 6:10 Your kingdom come. Your will be done, on earth as it is in heaven.

1 Corinthians 2:6-16 Yet among the mature we do speak wisdom, though it is not a wisdom of this age or of the rulers of this age, who are doomed to perish. But we speak God's wisdom, secret and hidden, which God decreed before the ages for our glory. None of the rulers of this age understood this; for if they had, they would not have crucified the Lord of glory. But, as it is written,

"What no eye has seen, nor ear heard, nor the human heart conceived, what God has prepared for those who love him"—these things God has revealed to us through the Spirit; for the Spirit searches everything, even the depths of God.

For what human being knows what is truly human except the human spirit that is within? So also no one comprehends what is truly God's except the Spirit of God. Now we have received not the spirit of the world, but the Spirit that is from God, so that we may understand the gifts bestowed on us by God. And we speak of these things in words not taught by human wisdom but taught by the Spirit, interpreting spiritual things to those who are spiritual.

Those who are unspiritual do not receive the gifts of God's Spirit, for they are foolishness to them, and they are unable to understand them because they are spiritually discerned. Those who are spiritual discern all things, and they are themselves subject to no one else's scrutiny.

"For who has known the mind of the Lord so as to instruct him?"

But we have the mind of Christ.

No Longer Mere Men

Paul rebuked the Corinthians for continuing to act like *"mere humans."* They were now expected to act as heavenly minded people. They were no longer to think according to human wisdom, but according to heavenly wisdom.

1 Corinthians 3:1-4 (NASB) Brothers and sisters, I could not address you as people who live by the Spirit, but as people who are still worldly—mere infants in Christ. I gave you milk, not solid food, for you were not yet ready for it.

Indeed, you are still not ready. You are still worldly. For since there is jealousy and quarreling among you, are you not worldly? Are you not acting like mere humans? For when one says, "I follow Paul," and another, "I follow Apollos," are you not mere human beings?

The book of James contrasts the behavior of earthly men with that of heavenly men, having *"wisdom from above." "Acting like mere men"* is marked by jealousy and quarreling. On the other hand, here is James' description of what it looks like to act as a *"man of heaven:"*

James 3:13-17 Who is wise and understanding among you? Show by your good life that your works are done with gentleness born of wisdom. But if you have bitter envy and selfish ambition in your hearts, do not be boastful and false to the truth. Such wisdom does not come down from above, but is earthly, unspiritual, devilish.

For where there is envy and selfish ambition, there will also be disorder and wickedness of every kind. But the wisdom from above is first pure, then peaceable, gentle, willing to yield, full of mercy and good fruits, without a trace of partiality or hypocrisy.

God, help us to live and act as heavenly people, and not mere men, so that when people see us, they see heaven! Notice that the wisdom of *"mere men"* is called earthly, unspiritual, and devilish. The wisdom of *"mere men"* is satanic. It is opposed to the power and purposes of God.

Chapter Six—Dead To The Earthly Man, Resurrected As A Man Of Heaven

Peter spoke to Jesus as a *"mere man,"* with his mind set on earthly things. To a human mindset, what Peter said was reasonable, but Jesus responded *"get behind me Satan!"*

Matthew 16:21-23 From that time on, Jesus began to show his disciples that he must go to Jerusalem and undergo great suffering at the hands of the elders and chief priests and scribes, and be killed, and on the third day be raised. And Peter took him aside and began to rebuke him, saying, "God forbid it, Lord! This must never happen to you." But he turned and said to Peter, "Get behind me, Satan! You are a stumbling block to me; for you are setting your mind not on divine things but on human things."

If we think and act according to heavenly wisdom, we will be sure to offend those who think like *"mere humans."* Heavenly wisdom seems foolish to them. Yet like Jesus, we must be firm in our purpose. We refuse to be moved by those who are earthly-minded and not heavenly-minded.

Put Off The Earthly Man And Put On The Man Of Heaven

God's will is for us to be conformed to the image of Christ, the man of heaven. This is our destiny. Christ was the firstborn among many brothers, who are heavenly people just as he is.

Romans 8:29 (NIV) For those God foreknew he also predestined to be conformed to the image of his Son, that he might be the firstborn among many brothers and sisters.

Hebrews 2:11 For the one who sanctifies and those who are sanctified all have one Father. For this reason Jesus is not ashamed to call them brothers and sisters

Colossians 3 continues to exhort us to put off the old man and put on the new man in Christ. The Holy Spirit is working to conform us to the image of Jesus so that we will love with the love of heaven, radiate the joy of heaven, carry the peace of heaven, and exercise the dominion of heaven— as those who are seated with Christ in heavenly places.

The world is in urgent need of heavenly people. Determine that whatever it takes, you will learn to live, act, think, and talk as a heavenly person. Let the fact sink into your spirit that this is your new identity in Christ. Walk on this earth with your head held high, possessed by the love of God, demonstrating the nature of Jesus, the man of heaven.

Colossians 3:5-17 Put to death, therefore, whatever in you is earthly: fornication, impurity, passion, evil desire, and greed (which is idolatry). On account of these the wrath of God is coming on those who are disobedient. These are the ways you also once followed, when you were living that life. But now you must get rid of all such things—anger, wrath, malice, slander, and abusive language from your mouth.

Do not lie to one another, seeing that you have stripped off the old self with its practices and have clothed yourselves with the new self, which is being renewed in knowledge according to the image of its creator. In that renewal there is no longer Greek and Jew, circumcised and uncircumcised, barbarian, Scythian, slave and free; but Christ is all and in all!

As God's chosen ones, holy and beloved, clothe yourselves with compassion, kindness, humility,

Chapter Six—Dead To The Earthly Man, Resurrected As A Man Of Heaven

meekness, and patience. Bear with one another and, if anyone has a complaint against another, forgive each other; just as the Lord has forgiven you, so you also must forgive. Above all, clothe yourselves with love, which binds everything together in perfect harmony. And let the peace of Christ rule in your hearts, to which indeed you were called in the one body.

And be thankful. Let the word of Christ dwell in you richly; teach and admonish one another in all wisdom; and with gratitude in your hearts sing psalms, hymns, and spiritual songs to God. And whatever you do, in word or deed, do everything in the name of the Lord Jesus, giving thanks to God the Father through him.

Don't let the lies and accusations of the enemy get you to doubt your new identity as a heavenly person, or pull you back into walking as a *"mere human"* again. The old has died, the new is here! As you read, meditate, and act on these scriptures, you will be established in this new identity.

These truths will become facts to you. You are now a heavenly person. You live in heaven because you have been raised with Christ and are in the presence of God. Heaven is in you, because the Holy Spirit lives in you. When you understand this, a fierce determination will grip your heart to make everything around you like heaven!

7. Heavenly Realities
The Fullness Of God

We briefly looked at Ephesians chapter 1 concerning the implications of Christ's resurrection. This is one of the most glorious passages in scripture.

Ephesians 1:15-23 (KJV) Wherefore I also, after I heard of your faith in the Lord Jesus, and love unto all the saints, Cease not to give thanks for you, making mention of you in my prayers; That the God of our Lord Jesus Christ, the Father of glory, may give unto you the spirit of wisdom and revelation in the knowledge of him: The eyes of your understanding being enlightened; that ye may know what is the hope of his calling, and what the riches of the glory of his inheritance in the saints, And what is the exceeding greatness of his power to us-ward who believe, according to the working of his mighty power,

Which he wrought in Christ, when he raised him from the dead, and set him at his own right hand in the heavenly places, Far above all principality, and power, and might, and dominion, and every name that is named, not only in this world, but also in that which is to come: And hath put all things under his feet, and gave him to be the head over all things to the church, Which is his body, the fullness of him that filleth all in all.

Notice that this scripture again mentions the knowledge of the Lord. The spirit of wisdom and revelation is found in the knowledge of the Lord. Colossians says that all the treasures of wisdom and knowledge are hidden in Christ.

Colossians 2:2-3 I want their hearts to be encouraged and united in love, so that they may have all the riches of assured understanding and have the knowledge of God's mystery, that is, Christ himself, in whom are hidden all the treasures of wisdom and knowledge.

God wants to open the eyes of our hearts through the knowledge of Christ, so we can see and experientially know the heavenly realities which the gospel makes available to us. God has given his fullness to the church, and heaven is heaven because of the fullness of God. It's the reality found in his presence. Because we have full access to God's presence, we have access to everything that is in heaven.

If the church is the fullness of God, then the church should be heaven on earth. This will be manifested in an ever-increasing degree as the eyes of our hearts our opened, growing in the knowledge of the Lord and growing up in all things into Christ.

As Ephesians 3:19 says, to know the love of God that surpasses knowledge is to be filled with all of the fullness of God. Let's talk about some of these heavenly realities which are found in the knowledge of the Lord.

The Hope Of His Calling
The hope of his calling, which was spoken of in Ephesians chapter one, is again mentioned in chapter 4. It is the hope of his calling for us, so it is also the hope of our calling.

Chapter Seven—Heavenly Realities

Ephesians 4:4 There is one body and one Spirit, just as you were called to the one hope of your calling

We can see in scripture that the *"hope of our calling"* and the *"hope of God's glory"* are the same. This is clear when we read that we are called to God's glory.

1 Peter 5:10 And after you have suffered for a little while, the God of all grace, who has called you to his eternal glory in Christ, will himself restore, support, strengthen, and establish you.

Scripture also speaks of certain aspects of being called to glory. We are called to repay evil with blessing and to inherit blessing.[111] We are called to endure when we suffer for doing right.[112] We are called out of darkness and into God's marvelous light.[113] We are called to eternal life.[114] (Which is knowing God.) We are called to peace.[115] We are called to freedom.[116] We are called into fellowship with Jesus.[117] We are called to be saints,[118] and called to belong to Jesus.[119]

Because of God's calling, we have a hope that will not disappoint us. This hope is the Holy Spirit dwelling in us, by which God's love (glory) has been poured out in our hearts.

Romans 5:1-5 Therefore, since we are justified by faith, we have peace with God through our Lord Jesus Christ,

---

[111] 1 Peter 3:9
[112] 1 Peter 2:20-21
[113] 1 Peter 2:9
[114] 1 Timothy 6:12
[115] Colossians 3:15, 1 Corinthians 7:15
[116] Galatians 5:13
[117] 1 Corinthians 1:9
[118] 1 Corinthians 1:2, Romans 1:7
[119] Romans 1:6

through whom we have obtained access to this grace in which we stand; and we boast in our hope of sharing the glory of God.

And not only that, but we also boast in our sufferings, knowing that suffering produces endurance, and endurance produces character, and character produces hope, and hope does not disappoint us, because God's love has been poured into our hearts through the Holy Spirit that has been given to us.

Notice that the New Revised Standard Version says we rejoice in the hope of sharing in God's glory. Yet what the text literally says is that we rejoice in the hope of God's glory. Look at Young's Literal Translation, for example:

Romans 5:2 (YLT) "through whom also we have the access by the faith into this grace in which we have stood, and we boast on the hope of the glory of God."

We already share in God's glory! If we read it literally, Romans 5:2 is not only a promise of something future. The glory of God which we have already experienced and partaken of gives us hope and confidence.

It is evident in Jesus' prayer to the Father that we are already partakers in God's glory. It is also evident in Paul's prayer for the Ephesians, since it is through the riches of God's glory that we are presently being strengthened in our inner beings.

John 17:22 The glory that you have given me I have given them

Ephesians 3:16 I pray that, according to the riches of his glory, he may grant that you may be strengthened in your inner being with power through his Spirit...

Chapter Seven—Heavenly Realities

We have been given the same glory that the Father gave Jesus. However, we're growing in the knowledge of the Lord. This means that as long as we continue to hold fast to Christ, there is far greater revelation of God's glory in our future than we have previously experienced.

There is also a new and glorious body which we will receive in a bodily resurrection. Christ in us is the hope of glory, because it is by the spirit of Christ in us that we know God's glory and it is manifested through us. Our hope is in the indwelling Spirit of Christ, who is able to do far more than all we could ask or imagine.

Colossians 1:27 To them God chose to make known how great among the Gentiles are the riches of the glory of this mystery, which is Christ in you, the hope of glory.

Romans 8:18 I consider that the sufferings of this present time are not worth comparing with the glory about to be revealed to us.

2 Corinthians 4:19 For this slight momentary affliction is preparing us for an eternal weight of glory beyond all measure

Philippians 3:21 He will transform the body of our humiliation that it may be conformed to the body of his glory, by the power that also enables him to make all things subject to himself.

Hebrews teaches that we have a sure hope, and faith is being assured of the hope we have.

Hebrews 6:19-20 We have this hope, a sure and steadfast anchor of the soul, a hope that enters the inner shrine behind the curtain, where Jesus, a forerunner on our behalf, has entered, having become a high priest forever according to the order of Melchizedek.

Hebrews 11:1 Now faith is the assurance of things hoped for, the conviction of things not seen.

Remember what the *"inner shrine behind the curtain"* is? It's heaven itself. We have a hope that enters heaven itself. We enter heaven and partake of the Lord's glory. We have hope because we are in heaven and on earth at the same time. Part of holding fast to the truth of the gospel and walking as heavenly people is standing on the confession of our hope. We hold fast to the heavenly realities found in the glory of God which fills heaven.

Hebrews 10:27 Let us hold fast to the confession of our hope without wavering, for he who has promised is faithful.

Romans 8 describes this sure and glorious hope which we have been given.

Romans 8:28-39 We know that all things work together for good for those who love God, who are called according to his purpose. For those whom he foreknew he also predestined to be conformed to the image of his Son, in order that he might be the firstborn within a large family. And those whom he predestined he also called; and those whom he called he also justified; and those whom he justified he also glorified.
    What then are we to say about these things? If God is for us, who is against us? He who did not withhold his own Son, but gave him up for all of us, will he not with him also give us everything else? Who will bring any charge against God's elect? It is God who justifies. Who is to condemn? It is Christ Jesus, who died,

Chapter Seven—Heavenly Realities

yes, who was raised, who is at the right hand of God, who indeed intercedes for us. Who will separate us from the love of Christ? Will hardship, or distress, or persecution, or famine, or nakedness, or peril, or sword? As it is written,

> *"For your sake we are being killed all day long; we are accounted as sheep to be slaughtered."*

No, in all these things we are more than conquerors through him who loved us. For I am convinced that neither death, nor life, nor angels, nor rulers, nor things present, nor things to come, nor powers, nor height, nor depth, nor anything else in all creation, will be able to separate us from the love of God in Christ Jesus our Lord.

It's important to understand how real this is. It's not just a theory, but has been proven in the hardest of times. Nothing can take away the heavenly reality we have been given in Christ. In another excerpt from Corrie Ten Boom's book, *"The Hiding Place,"* she relates her application of this scripture while in the Ravensbrück Concentration Camp. She and her sister experienced the reality of heaven even while in a place that seemed like hell on earth.

As for us, from morning until lights-out, whenever we were not in ranks for roll call, our Bible was the center of an ever-widening circle of help and hope. Like waifs clustered around a blazing fire, we gathered about it, holding out our hearts to its warmth and light. The blacker the night around us grew, the brighter and truer and more beautiful burned the word of God. "Who shall separate us from the love of Christ? Shall tribulation, or distress, or persecution, or famine, or nakedness, or peril, or sword? . . .

Nay, in all these things we are more than conquerors through him that loved us." I would look about us as Betsie read, watching the light leap from face to face. More than conquerors. . . . It was not a wish. It was a fact.

We knew it; we experienced it minute by minute—poor, hated, hungry. We are more than conquerors. Not "we shall be." We are! Life in Ravensbrück took place on two separate levels, mutually impossible. One, the observable, external life, grew every day more horrible. The other, the life we lived with God, grew daily better, truth upon truth, glory upon glory.[120]

Just as we have entered the heavenly reality of God's glory through the resurrection of Christ, it is through the resurrection of Jesus that we have been birthed into a living hope.

1 Peter 1:3-4 Blessed be the God and Father of our Lord Jesus Christ! By his great mercy he has given us a new birth into a living hope through the resurrection of Jesus Christ from the dead, and into an inheritance that is imperishable, undefiled, and unfading, kept in heaven for you...

We've explored the past, present, and future realities of salvation, and of God's resurrection power. First Peter states that our past resurrection with Christ, our new birth, gives us hope.

Paul also related his confidence in God's resurrection power presently working in him. As God, who raises the dead, continued to deliver him, his comfort and hope overflowed for the consolation and

---

[120] Boom, Corrie Ten; Elizabeth Sherrill; John Sherrill (2006-01-01). The Hiding Place (p. 206). Baker Publishing Group. Kindle Edition.

Chapter Seven—Heavenly Realities

salvation of the Corinthians. Obviously, *"salvation"* here is not speaking of salvation past, but of God's present deliverance.

2 Corinthians 1:3-10 Blessed be the God and Father of our Lord Jesus Christ, the Father of mercies and the God of all consolation, who consoles us in all our affliction, so that we may be able to console those who are in any affliction with the consolation with which we ourselves are consoled by God.

For just as the sufferings of Christ are abundant for us, so also our consolation is abundant through Christ. If we are being afflicted, it is for your consolation and salvation; if we are being consoled, it is for your consolation, which you experience when you patiently endure the same sufferings that we are also suffering. Our hope for you is unshaken; for we know that as you share in our sufferings, so also you share in our consolation.

We do not want you to be unaware, brothers and sisters, of the affliction we experienced in Asia; for we were so utterly, unbearably crushed that we despaired of life itself. Indeed, we felt that we had received the sentence of death so that we would rely not on ourselves but on God who raises the dead. He who rescued us from so deadly a peril will continue to rescue us; on him we have set our hope that he will rescue us again...

Paul was hard pressed in many ways. He had been at the end of his rope. He had even been stoned and left for dead once, but he got up, and went to another city the next day to preach the gospel.[121] That was the power of Christ working in him.

---

[121] Acts 14:19-20

Although my trials have not been nearly as severe as Paul's, I can relate to what he says here. I have been at the end of my rope more than once, feeling utterly, unbearably crushed. But God has always raised me up. God has raised me before and he will again. So my past experience with God's resurrection power gives me a sure hope and confidence in the present working of his resurrection power in whatever I may face. In everything, I am more than a conqueror through Christ's resurrection. It is a fact.

We also have hope stemming from the promise of a future bodily resurrection. It is not for this life only that we have hoped in Christ.

1 Corinthians 15:12-19, 30-32 Now if Christ is proclaimed as raised from the dead, how can some of you say there is no resurrection of the dead? If there is no resurrection of the dead, then Christ has not been raised; and if Christ has not been raised, then our proclamation has been in vain and your faith has been in vain. We are even found to be misrepresenting God, because we testified of God that he raised Christ—whom he did not raise if it is true that the dead are not raised.

For if the dead are not raised, then Christ has not been raised. If Christ has not been raised, your faith is futile and you are still in your sins. Then those also who have died in Christ have perished. If for this life only we have hoped in Christ, we are of all people most to be pitied...

And why are we putting ourselves in danger every hour? I die every day! That is as certain, brothers and sisters, as my boasting of you—a boast that I make in Christ Jesus our Lord. If with merely human hopes I fought with wild animals at Ephesus, what would I have gained by it? If the dead are not raised, "Let us eat and drink, for tomorrow we die."

Chapter Seven—Heavenly Realities

Here are the last words of Betsie Ten Boom, as she lay dying in the concentration camp. Betsie demonstrated heaven's reality where she was, and imparted an undying hope to those around her.

They placed the stretcher on the floor and I leaned down to make out Betsie's words, ". . . must tell people what we have learned here. We must tell them that there is no pit so deep that He is not deeper still. They will listen to us, Corrie, because we have been here."[122]

The hope we have because of Christ's resurrection gives us quite a different perspective than we would have if it was only for this life that we hoped in Christ. In the light of the resurrection, our sufferings become *"slight afflictions"* in comparison with the eternal weight of glory awaiting us.

Richard Wurmbrand, reflecting on his years of torture and persecution by communists, described God's perspective on the torture. He referred to Second Corinthians 4:17.

2 Corinthians 4:17 For this slight momentary affliction is preparing us for an eternal weight of glory beyond all measure

He explained that, from a human perspective, being tied to a cross and smeared with excrement is horrible. But to God, it's a *"slight affliction."* From a human perspective, fourteen years is a long time. To God, it's *"momentary."* If we understood the *"eternal weight of glory beyond all measure"* which these things were

---

[122] Boom, Corrie Ten; Elizabeth Sherrill; John Sherrill (2006-01-01). The Hiding Place (p. 227). Baker Publishing Group. Kindle Edition.

preparing us for, maybe we would better understand God's perspective.

Wurmbrand suggested that the Communist's horrible crimes, inexcusable to us, are lighter in God's eyes than they are in ours. Maybe their century of tyranny was only like a moment of erring astray in God's eyes. He was convinced that they could still be saved.[123]

Wurmbrand once referred to the question which Joshua asked an angel before he attacked Jericho. If someone were to ask him whether he was for the Communists or against them, he would reply in the same way as the angel did.

Joshua 5:13-14 (AMP) Now when Joshua was by Jericho, he looked up, and behold, a man was standing opposite him with his drawn sword in his hand, and Joshua went to him and said to him, "Are you for us or for our adversaries?" He said, "No; rather I have come now as captain of the army of the LORD.*"*

On one hand, Wurmbrand hated the system of communism. But in the spirit realm, he knew he was seated in heavenly places with Jesus. He explained that in heaven, the Communists are understood and loved in spite of their crimes, and angels are trying to help everybody to attain the highest goal of human life— to be like Christ.

Because he had a heavenly perspective, Richard Wurmbrand couldn't say that he was for or against the communists. However, he aimed to share God's love and

---

[123] Wurmbrand, Richard (2010-09-30). Tortured for Christ (Kindle Locations 1056-1062). Living Sacrifice Book Company. Kindle Edition.

Chapter Seven—Heavenly Realities

the gospel with them.[124] May we also see from a heavenly perspective and come to know, by experience, the love God has for even our enemies.

Releasing Hope

You are a heavenly person, and hope is one of the heavenly realities that you live in. You should exude hope. People who are suicidal should find the will to live again when they get near you.

On one of my trips to Russia, there was a sad and depressed old lady working in the hostel where I stayed. I went to Russia with the attitude that wherever I go is heaven. This lady said, *"When I see you, it makes me want to live again."*

As you grow in the knowledge of the Lord, holding fast to the truth of the gospel, you will abound and overflow with hope in every circumstance by the power of the Holy Spirit. You will become a wild optimist if you understand the realities of the gospel! Nothing can beat you! In everything, you are more than a conqueror through Christ!

Romans 15:13 May the God of hope fill you with all joy and peace in believing, so that you may abound in hope by the power of the Holy Spirit.

As a citizen of heaven and an ambassador of Christ,[125] you have authority to release heavenly hope. You can command and declare that the hope which is in heaven be established now on earth.

---

[124] Wurmbrand, Richard (2010-09-30). Tortured for Christ (Kindle Locations 981-986). Living Sacrifice Book Company. Kindle Edition.
[125] 2 Corinthians 5:20

Once I heard a sermon on Romans 15:13 and the Holy Spirit ingrained it in my spirit. By the time the sermon was over, I had it memorized. I went directly from that church to another place and laid my hands on many people there, saying *"In Jesus name, right now may the God of hope fill you with all joy and peace in believing, so that you may abound in hope by the power of the Holy Spirit."*

It's hard to put into words what happened, but it was heavenly! People were powerfully touched by the power of God and physically healed. Some fell down shaking and laughing. I spoke, and it happened.

Declare this heavenly reality with authority over people, and it will happen. As you understand the hope which you have been given, you can learn to declare *"Hope is the reality here now. Depression, hopelessness, discouragement, get out. Heaven is here now, because I am here, Christ is in me, and I am overflowing with hope."*

People will be delivered from heaviness and experience heaven now. Angels will often immediately minister when you declare this. Hope is another heavenly reality that will undo the works of the devil.

The Riches Of The Glory Of His Inheritance In The Saints

At the beginning of this chapter I quoted Ephesians 1:18, in which Paul prays that their eyes may be opened to know *"the riches of his glorious inheritance in the saints."* This phrase is usually interpreted in one of two different ways. The first is that we are God's inheritance. The second is that this is *"his inheritance"* in the sense that he is the giver of the inheritance, and so this is also our inheritance. No matter which interpretation you give

Chapter Seven—Heavenly Realities

to this scripture, both interpretations can be seen as true in other scriptures.

First, let's look at the truth that we are the Lord's inheritance. The Old Testament speaks in many places about Israel as the Lord's inheritance.

Deuteronomy 32:9 (KJV) For the LORD's portion is his people; Jacob is the lot of his inheritance.

Psalm 28:9 (KJV) Save thy people, and bless thine inheritance: feed them also, and lift them up forever.

Psalm 33:12 (KJV) Blessed is the nation whose God is the LORD; and the people whom he hath chosen for his own inheritance.

In the New Testament, we read that we are a holy nation, belonging to the Lord. We were grafted into God's holy nation when we put our faith in Christ.

1 Peter 2:9 (KJV) But ye are a chosen generation, a royal priesthood, an holy nation, a peculiar people; that ye should shew forth the praises of him who hath called you out of darkness into his marvelous light.

Understanding this should remind us how valuable and precious we are to the Lord. We are his treasure. We are the ones for which God gave his beloved Son. We are the *"joy"* for which Jesus endured the cross.

Hebrews 12:2 ...looking to Jesus the pioneer and perfecter of our faith, who for the sake of the joy that was set before him endured the cross, disregarding its shame, and has taken his seat at the right hand of the throne of God.

We can take this truth further to say that not only are we God's inheritance, but his inheritance is in us, because the Holy Spirit is in us. Look at the Young's Literal translation of Deuteronomy 32:9.

Deuteronomy 32:9 (YLT) For Jehovah's portion [is] His people, Jacob [is] the line of His inheritance.

"Jacob is the line of his inheritance," can imply that because Christ came from the lineage of Jacob, God's inheritance is Christ. God's inheritance is also in the saints, because Christ's spirit dwells in them.

It is by the empowerment of the indwelling spirit of Christ that we preach and demonstrate the gospel. As we minister by the power of the indwelling Holy Spirit, people are healed, delivered and born again. In this, the Father receives the reward for which he gave his Son; and Jesus receives the reward for which he suffered and died.

Part of the reason Jesus died was to make earth like heaven. Earth becomes like heaven through the empowerment of the Spirit of Christ dwelling in us. In this way, God's inheritance is in us.

Another part of God's inheritance is the creation which Christ came to redeem. As creation is set free by the power of Christ's spirit which dwells in us, the church presents to God his inheritance.

Romans 8:19, 21 For the creation waits with eager longing for the revealing of the children of God...that the creation itself will be set free from its bondage to decay and will obtain the freedom of the glory of the children of God.

Chapter Seven—Heavenly Realities

Our Inheritance

Now let's look at the second interpretation of Ephesians 1:18. Some see it as speaking of our inheritance in Christ. Several other scriptures in the New Testament talk about our inheritance. One of them is only a few verses before Ephesians 1:18.

Ephesians 1:11-14 (KJV) In whom also we have obtained an inheritance, being predestinated according to the purpose of him who worketh all things after the counsel of his own will: That we should be to the praise of his glory, who first trusted in Christ. In whom ye also trusted, after that ye heard the word of truth, the gospel of your salvation: in whom also after that ye believed, ye were sealed with that Holy Spirit of promise, which is the earnest of our inheritance until the redemption of the purchased possession, unto the praise of his glory.

The word *"earnest"* here means a pledge, in promise of the whole. It is because we have the Holy Spirit that we know we possess everything Jesus purchased with his blood. Let's look at what the Revised Standard Version says in verse 14:

Ephesians 1:14 (RSV) ...which is the guarantee of our inheritance until we acquire possession of it, to the praise of his glory.

When do we *"acquire possession"* of our inheritance? If the *"purchased possession"* is everything that Jesus bought with his blood; the acquiring of it is past, present, and future— just as salvation is. As Galatians 4 teaches, we have been made *"heirs of God."*

Galatians 4:1-7 My point is this: heirs, as long as they are minors, are no better than slaves, though they are the owners of all the property; but they remain under guardians and trustees until the date set by the father. So with us; while we were minors, we were enslaved to the elemental spirits of the world.

But when the fullness of time had come, God sent his Son, born of a woman, born under the law, in order to redeem those who were under the law, so that we might receive adoption as children. And because you are children, God has sent the Spirit of his Son into our hearts, crying, "Abba! Father!" So you are no longer a slave but a child, and if a child then also an heir, through God.

This is past. We have become heirs of the promises. We are no longer just minors, who are owners of the property, but not yet entrusted with it and so no better than slaves.

We also see the past aspect of coming into our inheritance in the typology of the Old Testament. Israel entered their inheritance, the Promised Land, after miraculously crossing the Red Sea and the Jordan River. Crossing the Red Sea was a type of water baptism. Crossing the Jordan is often considered to be a type of baptism in the Holy Spirit, or a type of the practical application of Christ's work to our lives.

After the crossing over comes entering into the inheritance. The Promised Land, Canaan, is also alluded to in several scriptures as paradise, God's garden, a new Eden.[126] It is symbolic of the heavenly realities the gospel has brought us into, paradise now.

Just as God gave the Promised Land to the Israelites but they had to take possession of it, we are to take possession of what Christ has bought for us with his

---

[126] For more information read this article:
http://www.templesecrets.info/jordan.html

Chapter Seven—Heavenly Realities

blood. This is our present inheritance. We read Ephesians 1:14, which says the Holy Spirit is the *"guarantee of our inheritance until we acquire possession of it."* In relation to our present inheritance which we acquire by actively appropriating God's promises, we could paraphrase Ephesians 1:14 like this: *"Because we have the Holy Spirit, we know all that God has given us, until we lay hold of it."*

This includes healing, deliverance, *"every spiritual blessing in heavenly places,"*[127] and *"everything we need for life and godliness."*[128] We have access to all this now, because Jesus purchased it for us.

Our present inheritance, which we are learning to possess, includes all the heavenly realities in the Father's presence. Because we have the *"guarantee"* of the Holy Spirit, we are able to see these realities to which we have been given access and to *"take possession"* of them.

1 Corinthians 2:9-12 But, as it is written, "What no eye has seen, nor ear heard, nor the human heart conceived, what God has prepared for those who love him"— these things God has revealed to us through the Spirit; for the Spirit searches everything, even the depths of God.

For what human being knows what is truly human except the human spirit that is within? So also no one comprehends what is truly God's except the Spirit of God. Now we have received not the spirit of the world, but the Spirit that is from God, so that we may understand the gifts bestowed on us by God.

It is by the Holy Spirit, who is the *"guarantee"* of our inheritance, that we understand God's gifts bestowed on us. This corresponds to Paul's prayer for the Ephesians

---

[127] Ephesians 1:3
[128] 2 Peter 1:3

that the eyes of their hearts be opened to understand their inheritance. God wants us to understand what we have been given in Christ, so that we will *"take possession"* of our inheritance, the Promised Land, heaven now. We *"redeem the purchased possession"* by redeeming God's *"promissory notes"* in scripture.

2 Peter 1:3-4 His divine power has given us everything needed for life and godliness, through the knowledge of him who called us by his own glory and goodness. Thus he has given us, through these things, his precious and very great promises, so that through them you may escape from the corruption that is in the world because of lust, and may become participants of the divine nature.

Hebrews 11:33 ...who through faith...obtained promises...

Hebrews 6:12 but imitators of those who through faith and patience inherit the promises.

2 Corinthians 1:19-22 For the Son of God, Jesus Christ, whom we proclaimed among you, Silvanus and Timothy and I, was not "Yes and No;" but in him it is always "Yes." For in him every one of God's promises is a "Yes." For this reason it is through him that we say the "Amen," to the glory of God. But it is God who establishes us with you in Christ and has anointed us, by putting his seal on us and giving us his Spirit in our hearts as a first installment.

All of these verses refer to *"redeeming"* God's promises as our inheritance, available for us in this life. The translation *"first installment"* which we see in the NRSV is from the same word translated *"earnest"* in the KJV.

Chapter Seven—Heavenly Realities

This passage in Second Corinthians 1 makes it clear that the inheritance of which the Holy Spirit is the *"guarantee"* or *"first installment,"* is not just something we will obtain after we die.

Our inheritance includes all the realities of heaven. We may possess them in this life by means of God's *"great and precious promises."* We have *"glorious riches"* available to us now!

It's not only to give us future hope that we must have the eyes of our hearts opened to understand the glorious riches of the inheritance God has given us. We must have our eyes opened as to see what we have access to in this life, so that we will take possession of it.

Philemon 1:6 (KJV) That the communication of thy faith may become effectual by the acknowledging of every good thing which is in you in Christ Jesus.

It's by acknowledging every good thing we have in Christ that the communication of our faith becomes effectual. God wants us to see our inheritance of every good thing which is in us by Christ, and he reveals it to us by the Holy Spirit so that we will make use of it.

The Holy Spirit is also a guarantee of the future aspect of our inheritance. It is the bodily resurrection, the *"redemption of our bodies."* Second Corinthians chapter five and Romans 8:23 both refer to this.

2nd Corinthians 5:1-5 For we know that if the earthly tent we live in is destroyed, we have a building from God, a house not made with hands, eternal in the heavens. For in this tent we groan, longing to be clothed with our heavenly dwelling—if indeed, when we have taken it off we will not be found naked. For while we are still in this tent, we groan under our burden, because we wish not to be unclothed but to be further clothed, so that what is mortal may be swallowed up by life. He who has prepared us for this very thing is God, who has given us the Spirit as a guarantee.

Romans 8:23 ...and not only the creation, but we ourselves, who have the first fruits of the Spirit, groan inwardly while we wait for adoption, the redemption of our bodies.

Understanding The Glorious Riches Of Our Present Inheritance

Acts 20:32 And now I commend you to God and to the message of his grace, a message that is able to build you up and to give you the inheritance among all who are sanctified.

Colossians 1:12 giving thanks to the Father, who has enabled you to share in the inheritance of the saints in the light.

1 Peter 1:3-4 Blessed be the God and Father of our Lord Jesus Christ! By his great mercy he has given us a new birth into a living hope through the resurrection of Jesus Christ from the dead, and into an inheritance that is imperishable, undefiled, and unfading, kept in heaven for you...

As in Ephesians 1:14, many have thought of this passage in First Peter as speaking only of a future inheritance which we are waiting for. Yet if we look more closely, we can see this not only applies to future promises and a glorified body, but also refers to *"every spiritual blessing in heavenly places,"* accessible now through God's *"great and very precious promises."*

Chapter Seven—Heavenly Realities

According to Strong's Greek Dictionary, the word translated *"kept"*[129] here means *"watched,"* especially in the sense of guarding or preserving. I looked at other places where this word is used in scripture, and a contextual examination confirms this. For example, it's used in several places in scripture in reference to *"keeping"* God's commandments. Where is this inheritance kept?

Ephesians 1:3 Blessed be the God and Father of our Lord Jesus Christ, who has blessed us in Christ with every spiritual blessing in the heavenly places

This inheritance is kept in heaven. Where are we seated with Christ? We are seated in heavenly places. God has blessed us in Christ with every spiritual blessing in heavenly places. Because we are in heaven, the fact that this inheritance is *"kept in heaven"* does not imply that we are waiting to receive it.

Rather, we understand that since these blessings are guarded in heaven, nothing on earth can take them from us. Nothing in this world can rob us of our joy or separate us from the Father's love. Nothing that is earthly can rob us of the heavenly reality which we have entered through the gospel.

Earlier, I mentioned how even when it seemed my house and natural possessions could be taken from me, I felt like the richest man in the world when I continued to lay my hands on people and see them healed. Yet healing is only one part of the inheritance we have been given in Christ. If you are in Christ, you are immeasurably wealthy with heavenly treasures that nothing on earth can take away or corrupt. What are these riches?

---

[129] Strong's Hebrew And Greek Dictionaries, word G5083

Luke 15:31 Then the father said to him, "Son, you are always with me, and all that is mine is yours..."

Just as the father in the parable of the prodigal son said to the older brother, our Father has given us everything! He has withheld nothing! Our relationship with the Lord is such that all we are belongs to him, and all that he has, he has given to us. This is the Father's magnanimous heart towards us!

Romans 8:32 He who did not withhold his own Son, but gave him up for all of us, will he not with him also give us everything else?

Jesus became poor so that by his poverty we might become rich– with heavenly, eternal, incorruptible riches. What love! In Christ we are immeasurably and gloriously rich.

2 Corinthians 8:9 But you know the generous act of our Lord Jesus Christ, that though he was rich, yet for your sakes he became poor, so that by his poverty you might become rich.

These spiritual treasures are the realities of heaven itself. God has given us the same glory that makes heaven what it is. We've been given the peace, joy, and love that fill heaven. Remember the scriptural promises that God has given us the same glory he gave to Christ[130] and has loved us with the same love he has for Christ.[131] If God did not withhold his own Son from us, what will he withhold?

---

[130] John 17:22
[131] John 17:23

Chapter Seven—Heavenly Realities

Numbers 18:20 (NKJV) I am your portion and your inheritance...

God has given us himself, along with every reality created by his presence! He himself is our inheritance, just as we are his! God has given you his fullness in Christ. How much richer could you be? Look carefully at these verses from Colossians. Notice how much is included in the fullness of God!

Colossians 1:15-19 He is the image of the invisible God, the firstborn of all creation; for in him all things in heaven and on earth were created, things visible and invisible, whether thrones or dominions or rulers or powers—all things have been created through him and for him. He himself is before all things, and in him all things hold together. He is the head of the body, the church; he is the beginning, the firstborn from the dead, so that he might come to have first place in everything. For in him all the fullness of God was pleased to dwell.

Colossians 2:9-10 For in him the whole fullness of deity dwells bodily, and you have come to fullness in him, who is the head of every ruler and authority.

Colossians 1:26-27 ...the mystery that has been hidden throughout the ages and generations but has now been revealed to his saints. To them God chose to make known how great among the Gentiles are the riches of the glory of this mystery, which is Christ in you, the hope of glory.

Colossians 2:2-3 I want their hearts to be encouraged and united in love, so that they may have all the riches of assured understanding and have the knowledge of God's mystery, that is, Christ himself, in whom are hidden all the treasures of wisdom and knowledge.

God wants our eyes to be opened to see what he has given us, so that we know we are immeasurably rich. This wealth will never run out, so we can keep on giving and giving. As we saw in Hebrews, we make use of this inheritance that is available to us by faith and perseverance, as we act on God's promises. We must understand what God has promised so that we can exercise faith and act on it.

We must come to know and believe how wealthy we are in him so that we will be continually giving his riches to the world. We will learn to have the attitude that *"I always have something to give."* We will walk like rich men when we see this, always having plenty from heaven to bless others. Rivers of living water will flow out of our innermost beings to the world.[132] This is the river of life,[133] by which the tree of life grows and the knowledge of the Lord multiplies!

When we see the radical generosity of Jesus, who became poor to make us rich, we will give our all to make others rich with the wealth of heaven. Paul expressed this attitude in his second letter to the Corinthians:

2 Corinthians 6:10 ...as sorrowful, yet always rejoicing; as poor, yet making many rich; as having nothing, and yet possessing everything.

The Immeasurable Greatness Of His Power To Us Who Believe

Paul wanted his readers to know *"the immeasurable greatness of his (God's) power to us who believe."* How

---

[132] John 7:38
[133] Revelation 22:21

Chapter Seven—Heavenly Realities

could this be stated in a stronger way? The passage goes on to talk about Jesus' resurrection and ascension, and our ascension with him. We have already talked about the implications that Christ's resurrection has for us. When we understand this and act on it, we will walk as heavenly people.

The reference in Ephesians 1 to the *"immeasurable greatness of God's power"* leads us to another one of Paul's prayers, recorded in Ephesians 3. We've already looked at this passage and seen how it is related to the knowledge of the Lord.

Ephesians 3:16-20 I pray that, according to the riches of his glory, he may grant that you may be strengthened in your inner being with power through his Spirit, and that Christ may dwell in your hearts through faith, as you are being rooted and grounded in love. I pray that you may have the power to comprehend, with all the saints, what is the breadth and length and height and depth, and to know the love of Christ that surpasses knowledge, so that you may be filled with all the fullness of God.

Now to him who by the power at work within us is able to accomplish abundantly far more than all we can ask or imagine, to him be glory in the church and in Christ Jesus to all generations, forever and ever. Amen.

If God's power that is at work in us is able to accomplish *"abundantly far more"* than all that we can ask or imagine, it is certainly able to accomplish what we can ask and imagine. Begin to ask God for great things and to imagine what his power can accomplish in and through you. Ask and believe for more than you ever have before!

I like to read stories of famous Christians and ponder the great things God did in their lives. Then I remind myself that they had weaknesses similar to mine.

Yet the same Spirit of God which accomplished such great things in their lives, lives in me!

I have heard of God's mighty deeds in the past. I desire to see the Lord do the same again, and even far more, through me! I don't want to only hear of God's mighty deeds at other times, in other places, and through other people. I want to participate in them, in my life, by his power at work in me.

Habakkuk 3:2 (NIV) Lord, I have heard of your fame; I stand in awe of your deeds, Lord. Repeat them in our day, in our time make them known

Jesus went to the Father, but we are on earth with his Spirit in us. Though we are on earth, heaven is in us because the Holy Spirit lives in us. It is because of this that Jesus said if we believed in him, we would do even greater works than he did!

John 14:12-14 Very truly, I tell you, the one who believes in me will also do the works that I do and, in fact, will do greater works than these, because I am going to the Father. I will do whatever you ask in my name, so that the Father may be glorified in the Son. If in my name you ask me for anything, I will do it.

Jesus was emphatic, saying, *"Very truly."* As hard as it may be for you to wrap your mind around the idea of your doing greater works than Jesus did while he walked the earth, take this as a fact and believe it. The Spirit of Christ within you is able.

In heaven there is never-ending increase. The manifestation of heaven which began in Jesus' earthly ministry will continue to grow through the church, his body, until it fills the whole earth.

Chapter Seven—Heavenly Realities

We see this in Daniel's prophesies. The *"stone that struck the statue"* in Daniel's prophesy was Jesus. That stone is becoming a great mountain and filling the earth as Jesus' body, the church, does the works of Jesus and grows up in all things into Christ.

Daniel 2:35 But the stone that struck the statue became a great mountain and filled the whole earth.

Daniel 2:44-45 And in the days of those kings the God of heaven will set up a kingdom that shall never be destroyed, nor shall this kingdom be left to another people. It shall crush all these kingdoms and bring them to an end, and it shall stand forever; just as you saw that a stone was cut from the mountain not by hands, and that it crushed the iron, the bronze, the clay, the silver, and the gold.

Matthew 3:2 ...the kingdom of heaven is at hand.

The same Holy Spirit that raised Christ from the dead lives in you and will give life to your mortal body. You will experience this in increasing measure as you grow in the knowledge of the Lord. The very power of Christ's resurrection is at work in you!

Romans 8:11 If the Spirit of him who raised Jesus from the dead dwells in you, he who raised Christ from the dead will give life to your mortal bodies also through his Spirit that dwells in you.

In First Samuel we read of the fearlessness and boldness Jonathan demonstrated because he trusted in God's power. This story should be an inspiration for us. Jonathan thought offensively when everyone else was cowering and hiding in holes from the Philistines.

1 Samuel 13:5-7 The Philistines mustered to fight with Israel, thirty thousand chariots, and six thousand horsemen, and troops like the sand on the seashore in multitude; they came up and encamped at Michmash, to the east of Beth-aven.

When the Israelites saw that they were in distress (for the troops were hard pressed), the people hid themselves in caves and in holes and in rocks and in tombs and in cisterns. Some Hebrews crossed the Jordan to the land of Gad and Gilead. Saul was still at Gilgal, and all the people followed him trembling.

Jonathan's thinking was totally different than everyone else's. He was in a different world than they were. Notice how he influenced his armor-bearer with his boldness. We should let ourselves be influenced by those who are confident in God's power.

1 Samuel 14:1, 4-10 One day Jonathan son of Saul said to the young man who carried his armor, "Come, let us go over to the Philistine garrison on the other side." But he did not tell his father...

In the pass, by which Jonathan tried to go over to the Philistine garrison, there was a rocky crag on one side and a rocky crag on the other; the name of the one was Bozez, and the name of the other Seneh. One crag rose on the north in front of Michmash, and the other on the south in front of Geba.

Jonathan said to the young man who carried his armor, "Come, let us go over to the garrison of these uncircumcised; it may be that the Lord will act for us; for nothing can hinder the Lord from saving by many or by few." His armor-bearer said to him, "Do all that your mind inclines to. I am with you; as your mind is, so is mine."

Chapter Seven—Heavenly Realities

Then Jonathan said, "Now we will cross over to those men and will show ourselves to them. If they say to us, 'Wait until we come to you,' then we will stand still in our place, and we will not go up to them. But if they say, 'Come up to us,' then we will go up; for the Lord has given them into our hand. That will be the sign for us."

It didn't matter that Jonathan and his armor-bearer were attacking the whole garrison by themselves. Nothing could hinder the Lord's victory. According to earthly strategy, it would have been an easier battle if the Philistines came down to them. Instead, Jonathan and his armor-bearer climbed up on their hands and knees to attack. By any natural wisdom, it would be almost impossible for them to overcome a garrison of soldiers from this position.

1 Samuel 14:11-15 So both of them showed themselves to the garrison of the Philistines; and the Philistines said, "Look, Hebrews are coming out of the holes where they have hidden themselves." The men of the garrison hailed Jonathan and his armor-bearer, saying, "Come up to us, and we will show you something."

Jonathan said to his armor-bearer, "Come up after me; for the Lord has given them into the hand of Israel." Then Jonathan climbed up on his hands and feet, with his armor-bearer following after him. The Philistines fell before Jonathan, and his armor-bearer, coming after him, killed them.

In that first slaughter Jonathan and his armor-bearer killed about twenty men within an area about half a furrow long in an acre of land. There was a panic in the camp, in the field, and among all the people; the garrison and even the raiders trembled; the earth quaked; and it became a very great panic.

Because of Jonathan's faith in God's power, the enemy panicked, the other Israelites who were hiding in holes came out and attacked, and a large army was routed. This was because of one man's faith.

Jonathan's faith must have encouraged the faith of his friend David, who wrote:

Psalm 18:28-29 "It is you who light my lamp; the Lord, my God, lights up my darkness. By you I can crush a troop, and by my God I can leap over a wall."

David was known for having mighty men around him who did amazing exploits. Here are some of their most outstanding feats.

1 Chronicles 11:11-14 This is an account of David's mighty warriors: Jashobeam, son of Hachmoni, was chief of the Three; he wielded his spear against three hundred whom he killed at one time.

And next to him among the three warriors was Eleazar son of Dodo, the Ahohite. He was with David at Pas-dammim when the Philistines were gathered there for battle. There was a plot of ground full of barley. Now the people had fled from the Philistines, but he and David took their stand in the middle of the plot, defended it, and killed the Philistines; and the Lord saved them by a great victory.

1 Chronicles 11:20 Now Abishai, the brother of Joab, was chief of the Thirty. With his spear he fought against three hundred and killed them, and won a name beside the Three.

Hebrews refers to these men and women, praising them for their faith. They are examples for us.

Chapter Seven—Heavenly Realities

Hebrews 11:33-34...who through faith conquered kingdoms, administered justice, obtained promises, shut the mouths of lions, quenched raging fire, escaped the edge of the sword, won strength out of weakness, became mighty in war, put foreign armies to flight.

Here is yet another scriptural reference to knowing God. Every Christian who knows their God will have the same attitude as Jonathan, David, and the mighty men of valor. We should expect to change the world!

Daniel 11:32 (KJV) ...the people that do know their God shall be strong, and do exploits.

We should become militant about dominating that which is around us, not with physical violence, but with the peace and goodness of God. We crush whatever is not in heaven. We crush hatred and fear with God's love. We crush torment— both mental and physical— because we carry the peace of God. We destroy evil with righteousness, undoing the works of the devil[134] wherever our feet take us. Let us bring heaven's reality wherever we go!

May we never intellectually limit what God can accomplish by his power which is at work in us! What we can accomplish, as we grow in the knowledge of the Lord, is far more than we could ever ask or imagine. His power is at work in you as you participate in his nature and share in his glory. His power is enough to complete the good work he has started in you[135] by conforming you to the image of Christ,[136] and it is enough to change the world around you.

---

[134] 1 John 3:8
[135] Philippians 1:6
[136] Romans 8:29

Present Access To Heaven

As you grow in the knowledge of the Lord and are strengthened in your innermost being by the power of the Holy Spirit, you will say with David *"By you I can crush a troop, and by my God I can leap over a wall."*[137]

---

[137] Psalm 18:29

8. Righteousness, Peace And Dominion

More Heavenly Realities

We've explored some of the heavenly realities of which the Apostle Paul wrote and also wove into his prayers. We could discuss many other such qualities; all aspects of God's glory.

The characteristics referred to as the *"fruit of the Spirit,"* are the reality of heaven. Each of them is a different aspect of God's nature. They stand in stark contrast to identifying marks of the old earthly man, to which we have died.

Galatians 5:19-24 Now the works of the flesh are obvious: fornication, impurity, licentiousness, idolatry, sorcery, enmities, strife, jealousy, anger, quarrels, dissensions, factions, envy, drunkenness, carousing, and things like these. I am warning you, as I warned you before: those who do such things will not inherit the kingdom of God.

By contrast, the fruit of the Spirit is love, joy, peace, patience, kindness, generosity, faithfulness, gentleness, and self-control. There is no law against such things. And those who belong to Christ Jesus have crucified the flesh with its passions and desires.

We have addressed some of these heavenly realities. They become evident in our lives and mark us as heavenly people as we grow in the knowledge of the Lord. The second book in this series will focus on the joy in God's presence, but now let's talk more about peace.

Peace And Salvation

I introduced the Greek word *"sozo"* in the first chapter. I noted that *"sozo"* is one of the words translated, *"salvation,"* but its meaning is practical and it is often used in the context of physical healing and deliverance.

I also compared every Old Testament use of *"shalom,"* the Hebrew word for peace. The contexts of many passages show that *"shalom"* is also a practical word. It's not a theoretical or spiritualized *"peace,"* but it touches every facet of our lives.

I concluded that the meaning of the Greek word for salvation, *"sozo,"* is very similar to the meaning of the Hebrew word for peace, *"shalom."* Isaiah is clear that Jesus paid the price for our peace. Peace is a heavenly reality that is included in our salvation.

Isaiah 53:5 (KJV) But he was wounded for our transgressions, he was bruised for our iniquities: the chastisement of our peace was upon him; and with his stripes we are healed.

Instead of literally *"the chastisement of our peace,"* the New Revised Standard Version says in this verse *"the punishment that made us whole."* This is from the word *"shalom"* in the text. It's interesting that in several places the King James Version translates the Greek word *"sozo"* in the same way that the NRSV translates shalom in Isaiah 53:5—as *"made whole."* This confirms what my contextual study seemed to show; the Old Testament

Chapter Eight—Righteousness, Peace And Dominion

word for peace and the New Testament word for salvation, have the same meaning.

This is significant; the reason that heaven is heaven is that the peace of God reigns there. The reason there is no sickness in heaven, is because the peace of God reigns. There is a heavenly order in the peace of God. Torment is not permitted.

The peace of God can enter every cell of a person's body and change the very structure and makeup of their body. When we understand the peace of God, we realize that not only does God heal, but he is healing. Wholeness is the reality that exists in heaven because of his presence.

Righteousness And Peace

Scripture teaches that peace comes through righteousness, and it is with the peace of God that we exercise dominion. Have you ever asked *"If Jesus really gave me authority to cast out demons and heal every sickness and disease, why isn't it working?"* I have found that to exercise the dominion God gave me as a heavenly person, I must be confident of having received his free gift of righteousness.

When we are not confident in our righteous identity in Christ, or are not walking according to it, our hearts condemn us and we are robbed of the peace which Christ purchased for us. This then hinders us from using the authority Christ gave us. When we hold fast to the truth of the gospel and walk in the heavenly reality of peace— that comes through justification and righteousness — then we exercise dominion in life. We dominate that which is around us with heaven's reality.

In Hebrews we see that King Melchizidek, who was a type of Jesus, is both the king of righteousness, and the king of peace. Consider this and these other scriptures which show how righteousness and peace go hand-in-hand.

Hebrews 7:2 His name, in the first place, means "king of righteousness;" next he is also king of Salem, that is, "king of peace."

Romans 5:1-2 Therefore, since we are justified by faith, we have peace with God through our Lord Jesus Christ, through whom we have obtained access to this grace in which we stand.

Isaiah 32:17 The effect of righteousness will be peace, and the result of righteousness, quietness and trust forever.

Psalm 85:10 (YLT) Righteousness and peace have kissed.

Peace And Your Dominion As A Man Of Heaven

Ephesians 6 talks about the armor of God. Part of this armor is the *"shoes of peace."*

Ephesians 6:15 As shoes for your feet put on whatever will make you ready to proclaim the gospel of peace.

Some people have said the *"sword of the Spirit"* is the only offensive weapon in the armor of God, but that is not true. The shoes that Roman soldiers wore were sometimes made with iron or brass, and often had long nails or spikes on the bottom. These served two purposes; they helped the soldier to stand his ground without slipping, and they were a dangerous weapon for trampling on the enemy. Romans 16:20 refers to this:

Chapter Eight—Righteousness, Peace And Dominion

Romans 16:20 (GW) The God of peace will quickly crush Satan under your feet

Imagine the Roman soldiers trampling their enemies with those spikes! Although it seems like an oxymoron, I have come to think of God's peace as a violent weapon. I don't mean *"violent"* in the sense of fighting flesh and blood, but forceful in crushing the works of Satan. In fact, the peace of God *"does violence"* to spirits of violence which work to destroy people.

We trample over all the power of the enemy with the peace of God. We exercise dominion by the peace which we obtain through righteousness. Here are three scriptures in which we can see the connection between peace and God's dominion.

Isaiah 9:6-7(KJV) For unto us a child is born, unto us a son is given: and the government shall be upon his shoulder: and his name shall be called Wonderful, Counselor, The mighty God, The everlasting Father, The Prince of Peace.

Of the increase of his government and peace there shall be no end, upon the throne of David, and upon his kingdom, to order it, and to establish it with judgment and with justice from henceforth even for ever. The zeal of the Lord of hosts will perform this.

Isaiah 60:17 I will appoint Peace as your overseer and Righteousness as your taskmaster.

Romans 14:17 For the kingdom of God is not food and drink but righteousness and peace and joy in the Holy Spirit.

If we have trouble exercising the dominion God has given us, it is usually because we are not at peace. These next two passages tell us what to do if God's peace is not reigning in our hearts. When we learn to do these things so God's peace reigns first in our hearts, then we will exercise the dominion of God's peace around us.

Philippians 4:4-9 Rejoice in the Lord always; again I will say, Rejoice. Let your gentleness be known to everyone. The Lord is near. Do not worry about anything, but in everything by prayer and supplication with thanksgiving let your requests be made known to God. And the peace of God, which surpasses all understanding, will guard your hearts and your minds in Christ Jesus.

    Finally, beloved, whatever is true, whatever is honorable, whatever is just, whatever is pure, whatever is pleasing, whatever is commendable, if there is any excellence and if there is anything worthy of praise, think about these things. Keep on doing the things that you have learned and received and heard and seen in me, and the God of peace will be with you.

1 John 3:18-22 Little children, let us love, not in word or speech, but in truth and action. And by this we will know that we are from the truth and will reassure our hearts before him whenever our hearts condemn us; for God is greater than our hearts, and he knows everything.

    Beloved, if our hearts do not condemn us, we have boldness before God; and we receive from him whatever we ask, because we obey his commandments and do what pleases him.

Romans 5 states we have peace and access to God's grace because of justification, which is the free gift of

Chapter Eight—Righteousness, Peace And Dominion

righteousness. This chapter continues to expound on exercising *"dominion in life"* through Jesus.

Through justification, grace exercises heaven's dominion, which is the peace of God. God's grace dominates. This leads to eternal life; the knowledge of the Lord filling the earth as the waters cover the seas, making earth like heaven.

Romans 5:17, 21 If, because of the one man's trespass, death exercised dominion through that one, much more surely will those who receive the abundance of grace and the free gift of righteousness exercise dominion in life through the one man, Jesus Christ...so that, just as sin exercised dominion in death, so grace might also exercise dominion through justification leading to eternal life through Jesus Christ our Lord.

Sometimes, when people needed help or healing, my heart condemned me. I felt bad about something. I had stumbled in some way, like doing or saying something that I regretted. At other times my heart was weighed down with anxiety. In order to exercise dominion to help these people, I needed to first face whatever was troubling me.

At such times, I've learned to remind myself of the justification and righteousness Jesus purchased for me with his blood. I get back up, making the decision to move on; putting off the old earthly man with its passions and lusts and putting on the heavenly man created in Christ's likeness. Then I exercise heaven's dominion to meet the need before me.

We grow in exercising dominion in life as we increasingly walk in God's peace. Whatever worries or fears you face, submit them to the perfect peace of God —received as you go to heaven now by approaching the Father. As you grow in the knowledge of the Lord and become continually aware of his presence, your peace will be great[138] and you can truly learn to *"be anxious for nothing."*[139] Scripture wouldn't tell us to do this if it weren't possible!

Anxiety is a form of fear, but perfect love casts out fear. Imagine what it would look like to live completely free from fear in this life! It's possible to operate free from all fear and anxiety, as a heavenly person, as you grow in the knowledge of the Lord.

If your life isn't free from anxiety right now, don't be discouraged! Rather, be encouraged by seeing the limitless possibilities in God's presence. You can grow in this. You will grow, because the Holy Spirit is working to conform you to the image of Christ, the heavenly man. Embrace the work of the Holy Spirit in your heart.

Even though God has given you dominion, you will not utilize that dominion over something you are so anxious about that it's obstructing your view of the Lord. Those who regularly exercise dominion in life are those who are continually looking into heaven and beholding the Lord's glory. When God's peace rules in your heart its dominion will extend through you to the people and circumstances around you.

Colossians 3:15 And let the peace of Christ rule in your hearts...

Worship Jesus and submit all anxiety to this perfect peace that passes understanding. All the peace in heaven is available to you now, as you boldly approach the Father to receive his mercy and grace. Let the peace and

---

[138] Isaiah 54:13
[139] Philippians 4:6

Chapter Eight—Righteousness, Peace And Dominion

goodness of God overwhelm you until you forget all fear and anxiety. Then crush the works of darkness.

Peace-Heaven's Reality

In Luke 10, we read of Jesus sending out his disciples to heal the sick and cast out demons, bringing them the Kingdom of Heaven. They were to use their words to release peace on the people they encountered. By doing so, they were offering them the reality of heaven.

Luke 10:5-6 Whatever house you enter, first say, 'Peace to this house!' And if anyone is there who shares in peace, your peace will rest on that person; but if not, it will return to you.

We're now going to look at Matthew 6:19 in two translations. These are more literal translations of this verse than many other versions are.

Matthew 6:19 (Phillips) I will give you the keys of the kingdom of Heaven; whatever you forbid on earth will be what is forbidden in Heaven and whatever you permit on earth will be what is permitted in Heaven!

Matthew 6:19 (YLT) and I will give to thee the keys of the reign of the heavens, and whatever thou mayest bind upon the earth shall be having been bound in the heavens, and whatever thou mayest loose upon the earth shall be having been loosed in the heavens.'

We first behold the heavenly reality created by God's presence. Then, we forbid on earth that which is forbidden in heaven, and we release on earth the reality and order that exist in heaven.

Say, for example, that a person named *"Bill"* has a problem with severe chronic pain and needs ministry.

Present Access To Heaven

I thank God for his presence and say *"In Jesus' name, may the peace of God fill Bill's body right now. May the peace and goodness of God touch every part of his being and fill every cell in his body, now! God, I thank you that your peace is driving out everything that is not in heaven. In Jesus' name, everything here that is not in the peace of God, get out now! May the peace of God dominate everything here right now, in Jesus' name. God, I thank you for the weight of your goodness resting on Bill right now, so he can feel it."*

I have done this more times than I can say. It feels like time suddenly stops and the most important thing in the world at that moment is the person in front of me. I am in heaven, and God's peace encompasses me. It's so strong that I sometimes weep. The person receiving ministry also often weeps.

Although the reality of God's presence is so real and overwhelming in that moment, it was available for me to walk in constantly. However, I only experienced it with such power when I turned my heart to the Lord and reminded myself of the truth of the gospel.

May I learn to walk continually in these heavenly realities, as a man of heaven, and with my mind always set on heavenly things! I thank God that his grace is working in me to teach and to help me to do so. I thank God that I am growing in Christ and am maturing so that there is a constant increase in my life!

Again and again, I have seen peoples' pain melt away as the peace of God filled their bodies. In some cases, years of chronic pain are crushed by the peace of God. Torment is ended.

I've felt people's tight and cramped muscles completely loosen and relax as God's peace filled their bodies. People often feel like a heavy weight just lifted off them. Sometimes their whole bodies get hot. I have felt almost mute at times, in awe of God and not wanting to speak because I have no words to express the glory we just experienced.

I particularly remember one old lady in Russia. As the peace of God filled her body, the pain disappeared; everything relaxed. She slumped into her chair until it looked like she was about to fall out! Even her skin became loose!

People often feel God's presence like a weight on their shoulders, heads, or hands. Sometimes bystanders feel a shiver go through their bodies. At times I have visited a house and the whole family felt the weight of God's glory. As they experience the weight of his glory, weights of oppression are lifted. Many people say they feel *"lighter."*

Dominating Your Environment With The Peace Of God

When the Israelites were about to enter the Promised Land, God told Joshua that everywhere he stepped was his possession. In the same way, we learn to claim everywhere we go as our turf and walk in the dominion of heaven. We carry the peace of God with us.

Joshua 1:3 Every place that the sole of your foot will tread upon I have given to you, as I promised to Moses.

My parents have lived in the city for many years. I also lived in the inner city when I was in the United States, and there was often crime or gang activity in the area. I determined that everywhere I went was mine, and the peace of God would rule there. I wrote scriptures on the walls of my basement and prayed that people who walked by my house or entered it would experience God's glory and be healed and delivered.

Present Access To Heaven

The place where my parents lived wasn't as dangerous as the neighborhood where I lived, but there were some bad neighborhoods nearby. Gang activity escalated, and some of my parents' neighbors were involved. One day my dad went out back and saw the word *"revolution"* spray painted on his back fence. He says that his spirit rose up and he declared *"There's not going to be any revolution here except that which is of the kingdom of God."*

The next day he went out and there was no sign of the graffiti. Nobody knew about it, and he could not even see any sign that it had been there but had been scrubbed away. This is exercising dominion in life, by the peace of God, through righteousness.

There was no revolution there, except for the kingdom of God coming to people. This neighborhood belonged to my dad; it was no gang's turf. Much ministry has happened at my parents' house, and I have often prayed for people there.

My parents started leaving things on their front bench to give away, and now their front bench is a place for the whole neighborhood to share with each other. People who pass by now also leave things like clothes or food there, and those who have a need take what they like. A spirit of generosity was released around them. They are exercising the dominion of God's peace in their neighborhood.

Here is another story from the life of Betsie Ten Boom, who demonstrated what it is like to walk as a heavenly person while suffering in a concentration camp. Even in this place that was like hell on earth, she exercised the dominion of heaven by releasing the peace of God. The barracks of the concentration camp where she lived were her territory, and the peace of God crushed the spirit of strife and anger.

Chapter Eight—Righteousness, Peace And Dominion

In Barracks 8 most of us had been Dutch. Here there was not even a common language and among exhausted, ill-fed people, quarrels erupted constantly. There was one raging now as the women sleeping nearest the windows slammed them shut against the cold. At once scores of voices demanded that they be raised again.

Brawls were starting all up and down that side of the room; we heard scuffling, slaps, sobs. In the dark I felt Betsie's hands clasp mine. "Lord Jesus," she said aloud, "send Your peace into this room. There has been too little praying here. The very walls know it. But where You come, Lord, the spirit of strife cannot exist...." The change was gradual, but distinct. One by one the angry sounds let up.

"I'll make you a deal!" The voice spoke German with a strong Scandinavian accent. "You can sleep in here where it's warmer and I'll take your place by the window!" "And add your lice to my own?" But there was a chuckle in the answer. "No thanks."

"I'll tell you what!" The third voice had a French burr. "We'll open them halfway. That way we'll be only half-frozen and you'll be only half-smothered." A ripple of laughter widened around the room at this. I lay back on the sour straw and knew there was one more circumstance for which I could give thanks. Betsie had come to Barracks 28.[140]

"Lights-out blew and the scramble into the bunks began. I hoisted myself to the middle tier and crawled across those already in place. What a difference since Betsie had come to this room! Where before this had been the moment for scuffles and cursing, tonight the

---

[140] Boom, Corrie Ten; Elizabeth Sherrill; John Sherrill (2006-01-01). The Hiding Place (p. 211). Baker Publishing Group. Kindle Edition.

huge dormitory buzzed with "Sorry!" "Excuse me!" And "No harm done!"[141]

What influence Betsie was able to have in such a horrible place by simply being constantly aware of God's presence and releasing the peace of God! May the work of the Holy Spirit in Betsie's life encourage you. God has given you the same Holy Spirit, and he is able to do immeasurably more than you could ever ask or imagine, according to his great power at work in you.

---

[141] Boom, Corrie Ten; Elizabeth Sherrill; John Sherrill (2006-01-01). The Hiding Place (p. 217). Baker Publishing Group. Kindle Edition.

9. Heavenly Minded
Set Your Minds On Things Above

God highlighted Colossians chapter 3 to me on my second trip to Russia. I was excited about this trip, expecting to see the Lord do great things. But on the second day of the trip, I became distressed and depressed with confusion over a relationship. In the past, I had spent too much time in the depths of despair and depression. Now I needed to stand my ground and not let myself be robbed of what God wanted to do.

As I was praying and reading scripture, I came to Colossians chapter 3. I could feel the words strengthening my spirit. The Lord spoke to me about two specific things through this passage, and especially through verses 1-3.

Colossians 3:1-3, 5, 9-10 Since, then, you have been raised with Christ, set your hearts on things above, where Christ is, seated at the right hand of God. Set your minds on things above, not on earthly things. For you died, and your life is now hidden with Christ in God...Put to death, therefore, whatever belongs to your earthly nature...you have taken off your old self with its practices and have put on the new self, which is being renewed in knowledge in the image of its Creator.

First of all, God corrected me, telling me to stand firm and cast depression aside. I had died to the earthly man that is subject to earthly things. I was not to be subject to earthly circumstances, but to heavenly reality. The heavenly reality was that in God's presence there is fullness of joy![142] If my mind was set on heavenly things, then it was impossible for me to stay depressed! I was to put off the earthly, depressed, self-centered man, and put on the new self, full of joy in the Lord's presence.

Although it seemed like it would be difficult, I obeyed and refused to be depressed. I was quickly filled with overflowing joy and peace.

Colossians 3:14-15 And over all these virtues put on love, which binds them all together in perfect unity. Let the peace of Christ rule in your hearts, since as members of one body you were called to peace. And be thankful.

By putting on love, I put off self-centeredness. My focus was no longer on myself. When I put on the heavenly reality of love, my joy now came from the love of God in my heart and was no longer dependent on earthly circumstances. It was no longer about me!

Having my joy rooted in love made it possible to have joy in any circumstance. I always have access to God's presence, and nothing can stop me from loving. As I walk in love, God will always freely give me what I need to meet other's needs.

I'm not saying that when we walk as heavenly people we don't feel emotions like sadness, or experience a healthy grieving process in time of loss. However, when we set our minds on heavenly things, we will not be disabled by those emotions or lose our joy. Our joy will not be contingent on our situation, but on being able to love. We will not be dominated by the pain we feel, because our focus is not on ourselves.

When we let emotional pain turn us inward to focus on self, we fall prey to self-pity and become earthly-minded. We stop loving and looking to the needs of others, and we become weak.

---

[142] Psalm 16:11

Chapter Nine—Heavenly Minded

I've found that the joy experienced by walking as a heavenly person is very real. It's sustained me in times of great grief or discouragement. I especially recall two difficult times when ministering healing to others in spite of great personal pain and discouragement helped me to keep going. Ministering to others kept me from turning totally inward and focusing on myself and my problems. As I let the Holy Spirit express God's love through me, I experienced heavenly joy that sustained me. It kept me from giving up and despairing.

The first of these trials was a pressing financial situation. I had a dispute with the IRS, which claimed I owed them a large sum of money. With penalties and interest, the amount was nearly all I had earned in one of the two years contended. When they put a tax lien on my house, I felt physically sick and couldn't sleep at night because of the anxiety. I felt very discouraged and helpless, like I was being robbed.

I did fall prey to self-pity for some time, and had moments of despair. When my thoughts became negative, my mom helped me by speaking the truth of scripture. I had to get up, keep looking to the Lord, and keep going. I didn't stop laying hands on the sick, and I saw beautiful miracles happen! Pain left, and surgery was cancelled. People wept as God's goodness tangibly overwhelmed them.

I knew that no money could buy these miracles. I saw God do wonders that no doctor could do. And so I found comfort in the fact that even if my house, all my money, and everything I had was stolen, nobody could take the Holy Spirit from me. I felt like the richest person in the world because I had the Holy Spirit, and God had given me something priceless to give to others. I was rich because I could lay my hands on people and they would be healed. I had a joy that came from walking in love— by giving to others the true riches which God had given me.

The second situation was the painful breakup with my Russian girlfriend, whom I thought I was going to marry. It was unexpected and unexplained, and occurred right before my third trip to Russia. I had bought an engagement ring and had planned to propose to her on that trip.

The grief was terrible, unlike anything else I have ever experienced. She had been my best friend. When she broke up with me, the grief was so intense that it felt like a hand reached into my belly and ripped out my stomach.

At the same time, it seemed like everything was working against my trip to Russia. When I applied for a needed document to get a three month visa, my year of birth was written as 1958 instead of 1985 and my name was grossly misspelled.

There was financial difficulty and pressure on every side, so that the trip seemed impossible. Yet I was absolutely determined to keep going and obey God. When my girlfriend broke up with me, I felt perplexed over the adversity. I wondered if I had somehow missed God, confusing my own desires with his voice.

But how could I have missed God's voice about going to Russia? On my first trip to Russia, though not expecting to ever return there again, I learned most of the Cyrillic alphabet on the second day. I barely even tried! At the end of that first two week trip, I could read the book of First John in Russian and understand it. (Although my pronunciation was poor.) On both trips God had performed amazing signs and miracles!

At the end of my first trip, I had felt a deep love for the people and the place around me. It became so strong that I felt currents of power, like liquid love, flowing from my hands and mouth. During the second trip, I was almost continually walking in heaven's reality. When I returned home from the second trip and told my parents about the miracles God had done, gold dust spontaneously appeared on my face and my mom's face. Many such things happened.

I had invested so much time in studying Russian, and I loved the people more than words could say. It would be heartbreaking not to go back, but I only wanted to obey the Lord. It would also be a difficult financial sacrifice to go on this trip.

Chapter Nine—Heavenly Minded

I went to a meeting where Dennis Balcombe, a famous missionary to China, was preaching. As I listened to him, I felt an overwhelming desire and a sense of urgency to go to Russia. However, I was still confused, not knowing if this desire was from the Lord or my own emotions. I stood there, crying out to God and weeping.

Then spontaneously, people came all around me. They got down on the ground and held my feet, praying for me. As the meeting ended, several people, independently of each other, told me that the Lord had led them to bless my feet. Later, yet another person approached me in the hallway and said, *"I know this sounds funny, but can I hold your feet and pray for you? I feel like God told me to bless your feet."*

Isaiah 52:7 How beautiful on the mountains are the feet of those who bring good news, who proclaim peace, who bring good tidings, who proclaim salvation, who say to Zion, "Your God reigns!"

The message was clear. God was sending me to Russia. Three days later, I again felt a consuming love for Russia and a great desire to go. This time the love became like a current of electricity, which I physically felt flowing through my whole body from head to toe. I knew that God had sent me. Since I was not able to get the three month visa, due to the errors and misspellings on other documents, I would stay for one month on a tourist visa and also try to spend time in Ukraine.

The trip to Ukraine worked out. I volunteered there at a children's home. It was normal for me to see healing miracles wherever I went, but no miracles happened in Ukraine. I did lay my hands on a few people, but I felt weak and helpless inside, and nothing happened.

In the intensity of my sorrow, I had lost my appetite, eating little for several weeks. I felt numb with pain and grief. However, I was with wonderful people, and I loved being with the children. That comforted me.

Present Access To Heaven

When I arrived in Russia, I wept aloud with the joy of being there again. I still felt intense grief, but there was also great joy to again see these people and this city I so dearly loved. There was no place in the world that I would rather be at that moment, and it felt like there was an army of angels with me. It was an indescribable feeling!

The mourning did not end then. I sobbed every day. I felt like I couldn't bear the pain, as if I had been torn in two. Never had I experienced such grief. There were times when I had the darkest of thoughts. I remember one day I got lost in the city and the devil spoke to me about killing myself.

They were not my thoughts but the wiles of the enemy. He wanted me to think that they were my thoughts. I refused suicide as a selfish thing—as believers we are not to live only for ourselves but for others. You don't have anything to give if you are dead. I repeatedly had to refuse to only focus on myself and choose to turn to the Lord instead.

Yet when I was with the people, my emotions were overwhelmed with love for them and with thankfulness to God for being able to be in Russia again. There was nowhere else in the world I would rather be, and it felt like all of heaven was backing me! It was pure grace.

As I worshiped the Lord, the love I felt became like a current of power flowing through my body. Again, I became so aware of God's love that I could tangibly feel it in the air around me. That power touched various parts of my body, indicating where the people around me had physical problems.

I also saw mental pictures, or felt a wind touch part of my body, and understood how people needed healing. The wind was the ministry of angels. (A topic we will examine in the second book of this series.)

I shared the things I felt, and the people with those issues were healed— many without me even touching them. I particularly remember an old Jewish lady at a Jewish culture club. God showed me her issue in three ways: I saw a picture in my mind of a large tumor or cyst in someone's abdominal

Chapter Nine—Heavenly Minded

area; I felt a wind blow on my abdomen; and I felt a vibration touch me there.

I learned that she had a large growth in her abdomen, which caused great pain. I told her *"Don't worry. God is healing you, and next time I see you, it won't be there."* Two weeks later I saw her and it had disappeared.

I was filled with such immense joy when I saw the healings that I jumped! Nobody would have imagined that only a few hours before I'd been sobbing with grief, and that when I went home I would be sobbing with grief again! But God's presence—heaven—was there. It was accessible to me, no matter what my natural situation. I experienced heaven even in the midst of the greatest grief I had ever known.

The reality that is in God's presence never changes, no matter what the natural circumstance. Heaven is always here and is always accessible. The devil would like to deceive us into focusing on ourselves and living in a lesser reality than what God has made available.

Rejecting Self-Pity

In writing this, I don't mean to be insensitive to the struggles and trials that others face. Some of you have experienced much more affliction than I have. Yet even in the midst of the greatest pain and opposition, there are people who've proven it's possible to experience heavenly joy by focusing on loving others instead of on our own pain or loss.

Several times, I've referred to Richard Wurmbrand's story of suffering in Communist dungeons and torture chambers. If anyone had an excuse to wallow in self-pity, he did. I'm not saying that he didn't have some very dark times, because he did. But as I read his book, it's evident that he had great joy in sharing the gospel and love of Christ with everyone in prison, even his torturers.

His focus moved from his own troubles to meeting the needs of others. He let God's love for others flow through him. This enabled him to keep going despite the horrors, instead of despairing and giving up. Doctors who saw him after he was

Present Access To Heaven

released from prison said that it was a miracle he survived such an ordeal.

Corrie and Betsie Ten Boom also had plenty of reason to feel sorry for themselves. At times Corrie did struggle with self-pity, and her sister Betsie was a great example to encourage her. Here is another quote from Corrie, talking about her sister Betsie when they were in a Nazi prison in Holland.

I had the feeling she was as content to be reading the Bible here in Vught to those who had never heard it as she'd been serving soup to hungry people in the hallway of the Beje.[143]

Betsie's focus wasn't on where she was or what would happen to her. She was so focused on ministering to others that she was content even in prison. She was participating in the love and nature of God. As she did, rivers of living water flowed. She walked as a heavenly person.

When she was in the Ravensbrück concentration camp, Betsie had a vision of a beautiful home where they would help people who'd suffered to forgive and love again. She overflowed with a joy that could never be taken from her. Her joy sprang from the love in her heart, which she was constantly receiving from the heavenly reality of God's presence. She didn't think of herself first, but of others.

And as we prayed, God spoke to us about the world after the war. It was extraordinary; in this place where whistles and loudspeakers took the place of decisions, God asked us what we were going to do in the years ahead.

Betsie was always very clear about the answer for her and me. We were to have a house, a large one— much larger than the Beje— to which people who had been damaged by concentration-camp life would come until they felt ready to live again in the normal world. "It's such a beautiful house,

---

[143] Boom, Corrie Ten; Elizabeth Sherrill; John Sherrill (2006-01-01). The Hiding Place (p. 195). Baker Publishing Group. Kindle Edition.

Chapter Nine—Heavenly Minded

Corrie! The floors are all inlaid wood, with statues set in the walls and a broad staircase sweeping down. And gardens! Gardens all around it where they can plant flowers. It will do them such good, Corrie, to care for flowers!"

I would stare at Betsie in amazement as she talked about these things. She spoke always as though she were describing things that she saw— as if that wide, winding staircase and those bright gardens were the reality, this cramped and filthy barracks the dream.[144]

Here are some of Betsie's dying words. She refused to wallow in self-pity. Even with her last breaths, she dreamed about how she could show the love of God to others. She was excited about it!

"A camp, Corrie— a concentration camp. But we're . . . in charge . . ." I had to bend very close to hear. The camp was in Germany. It was no longer a prison, but a home where people who had been warped by this philosophy of hate and force could come to learn another way. There were no walls, no barbed wire, and the barracks had window boxes.

"It will be so good for them . . . watching things grow. People can learn to love, from flowers. . . ." I knew by now which people she meant. The German people. I thought of The Snake standing in the barracks door that morning. "State your number. All prisoners must report for the count."

I looked into Betsie's shrunken face. "We are to have this camp in Germany instead, Betsie? Instead of the big house in Holland?" "Oh no!" she seemed shocked. "You know we have the house first! It's ready and waiting for us . . . such tall, tall windows! The sun is streaming in—" A coughing fit seized her; when finally she lay still, a stain of blood blackened the straw. She dozed fitfully during the day and night that followed,

---

[144] Boom, Corrie Ten; Elizabeth Sherrill; John Sherrill (2006-01-01). The Hiding Place (pp. 222-223). Baker Publishing Group. Kindle Edition.

waking several times with the excitement of some new detail about our work in Holland or Germany.[145]

Everything Betsie described came to pass— except that only Corrie survived the concentration camp to experience it. After Corrie's miraculous release, a Dutch woman gave her a house in Holland exactly like the one Betsie described. Later, the Germans gave Corrie a concentration camp to be turned into a place of ministry and healing. They took down the walls and barbed wire, put window boxes on the windows, and planted flowers.

It might sound crazy to talk about putting off the earthly man and putting on the man of heaven, full of joy in the Lord's presence, no matter the circumstances. This is why I deemed it necessary to share the stories of Christians who suffered greatly and still walked as heavenly people. I want to be clear that even in situations much worse than I have faced, this isn't only a nice theory but is truth that can be put into practice.

I have functioned in this reality to a small degree, but I want to walk in it much more. Stories like Betsie's show me it's possible to walk as a heavenly person even when it seems like hell is all around. If Betsie refused to wallow in self-pity even in such circumstances, and instead chose to give heavenly riches to those around her, I must do the same. When I remember her, I am challenged to put off the earthly, self-centered man and to put on the man of heaven, which loves like God loves.

Making The Maimed Whole

Let's revisit my second trip to Russia. The first thing the Lord told me that day when I read Colossians 3 was that I needed to put off the self-centeredness and earthly-mindedness that made me subject to depression. The second was that I needed to stop being earthly-minded by withdrawing from laying hands on

---

[145] Boom, Corrie Ten; Elizabeth Sherrill; John Sherrill (2006-01-01). The Hiding Place (pp. 226-227). Baker Publishing Group. Kindle Edition.

Chapter Nine—Heavenly Minded

maimed people, even though I laid hands on others who were sick or injured.

I was laying hands on many sick and injured people, but I avoided laying hands on those who had missing body parts. It felt too scary, too intimidating. This was earthly-minded. I wasn't supposed to be earthly-minded, because I had been raised with Christ as a man of heaven.

It was no more difficult for God to create new body parts than it was for him to heal a headache. God didn't want to do it any less—if anything he would want to do it even more! So the only reason I avoided laying hands on people with missing limbs was that I was thinking carnally instead of having my mind set on heaven. If Jesus did it, so should I.

Matthew 15:30-31(KJV) And great multitudes came unto him, having with them those that were lame, blind, dumb, maimed, and many others, and cast them down at Jesus' feet; and he healed them: Insomuch that the multitude wondered, when they saw the dumb to speak, the maimed to be whole, the lame to walk, and the blind to see: and they glorified the God of Israel.

I decided to repent of this earthly-mindedness and from yielding to intimidation in this area. I began to approach people who were missing legs to minister to them, even though it felt like my heart was in my throat!

The first guy I remember laying hands on was a man in the metro with both of his legs blown off. I explained to him how God healed me, and that I believed God would like to make his legs grow again and it would be possible if I would believe. I explained how I had been growing in faith and seeing many miracles happen, and that I would like to see still greater miracles happen.

He was happy to let me put my hand on his shoulder, and I commanded the legs to grow back in Jesus' name. I didn't see anything happen then, and have no way of knowing if the man's legs eventually grew back, but he kept coming back to me again and again to thank me. He came again in the metro

Present Access To Heaven

train and thanked me. So I wondered if he had felt something, and it was an encouraging experience!

I continued to lay my hands on people no matter what the condition. Many healing miracles happened throughout that trip. Then I returned from Russia and spent a few days in New York City. When I left, my girlfriend went to another city in Russia, Chelyabinsk, to visit her mother. Chelyabinsk is a ten time zone difference from New York and is in the Asian part of Russia.

She called me when I was in New York, telling me that her mother had caught her finger in a heavy door and severed about 5 centimeters of the finger. They were unable to reattach it. So on the phone we prayed and I said *"In Jesus' name, we command the finger to grow back."*

Two months later my girlfriend visited her mother again. The finger was growing back, with a new fingernail forming! She returned about a month later, and the finger had all grown back. Her mother was an atheist, so I thought this should convince her that God is real.

My girlfriend told her mother *"Mom, we prayed for you. This is a miracle."* But her mother said *"No, the doctor told me that there is a seed in my finger. He said I was lucky and cut it off where the seed was, and so it activated the seed and made my finger grow again."*

I wasn't able to find any scientific basis to the idea of a *"seed"* in the finger. I asked a friend who is a doctor in the US if that story made any sense to him. It didn't. I think the Russian doctor may have been an atheist as well and tried to come up with a natural explanation for something that couldn't be explained naturally. (Rather than acknowledging a miracle.)

I was thrilled by the finger growing back. I was experiencing the reality of heaven to a greater degree as I grew in the knowledge of the Lord and acted upon his word.

Not long after that, I took a trip to New York City to visit Polish friends. A Polish lady had a leg missing, as well as severe *"phantom pain"* and other health issues. She said with

Chapter Nine—Heavenly Minded

tears *"I know God must have a reason for making me suffer so much, but I don't know if I can bear it any longer."*

I was stirred in my spirit and told her that Jesus healed all who came to him, and that Jesus is the image of the invisible God and is the same yesterday, today, and tomorrow. God did not want her suffering with the phantom pain!

I explained that Jesus had ascended and given us the Holy Spirit, saying we would do the same works as he did and even greater works. The church is the body of Christ on earth, and God works his will through us. We are growing up into all the fullness of the measure of the stature of Christ.

Therefore, if she wasn't yet healed, it wasn't because God didn't want to heal her or even that he was waiting to heal her. Rather, it was because we as the church had not yet grown up into all that Christ is.

Then I told her, *"If Jesus has his way through me right now, you can have your leg back."* I said this very matter-of-factly, because it was fact to me. But when I said it, she abruptly yelled, interrupting me, grabbed my hand, and put it on the stump of her leg. I was confused for a minute. A friend was interpreting for me, since my Polish was not very good.

I asked what happened, and the lady explained that she had yelled *"it's reacting"* because when I said *"If Jesus has his way through me right now, you can have your leg back,"* the stump of her leg began to violently vibrate. She interrupted me, grabbing my hand and putting it on the stump, so that I could feel how it was shaking and vibrating!

I then prayed for her and blessed her, and several other people were healed after that. For some time, I wondered if her leg would grow over time like the finger did. However, I will be honest. When I later spoke to my Polish friend who had been interpreting, the lady was still missing her leg.

Even though the lady's leg didn't grow back yet, the manifestation was exciting because I knew that I was growing in Christ and this was possible! If a finger grew back, why not a leg? If Jesus made the maimed whole, should we not do the same?

In the next book, I will relate how my brother and I laid hands on a blind lady and she felt God's power, yet had only slight improvement. I later testified of this, thanking God for the slight improvement and the manifestation of his power. My sister's eyes were instantly healed as I spoke.

I didn't focus on the fact that the blind lady still wasn't seeing fully, but I thanked God for what he was doing. In the same way, as I share the story of the Polish lady with no leg, I rejoice in the manifestation that I know was from God.

I do my best to never exaggerate these accounts, but to relate them as accurately as possible. I don't lie, but I do share what has happened and I thank God for it. If a person felt God's goodness and power when I prayed for them, even if full healing wasn't yet manifested, should I not thank God for his work rather than focusing on what hasn't happened yet?

2 Corinthians 4:18 So we fix our eyes not on what is seen, but on what is unseen, since what is seen is temporary, but what is unseen is eternal.

After that experience, I touched the hand of a man who had no finger and said *"finger grow back, in Jesus' name."* Although I'm not aware of it having grown back since, he instantly felt the physical sensation that it was there, which he had not felt in years. But we didn't see it!

Some might think that it seems foolish or pointless for me to rejoice in such a manifestation since we still didn't see a finger. It is not! When we are learning to walk in heavenly wisdom and in faith, it will seem foolish to the naturally minded.

1 Corinthians 1:25 For the foolishness of God is wiser than human wisdom, and the weakness of God is stronger than human strength.

Some might say *"If God was going to give him a finger, he would do it all the way! God doesn't do things halfway."* Such

Chapter Nine—Heavenly Minded

a statement shows a lack of understanding of how God works. The immeasurable greatness of his power for us who believe is *"according to his power that is at work within us."*[146] God works through us; through the church which is his body, as we grow in the knowledge of him. We are growing up in all things *"into the full measure of the stature of Christ."*[147]

Yes, I have a lot of room to grow. And growing is an exciting thing! When I share my stories, I don't present my life as a perfect picture of what it looks like to walk as a *"man of heaven."* Jesus has modeled that. I'm only sharing the experiences I have had while learning to put these scriptural truths into practice. I tell my history of growing in truth, and I hope it will encourage you to grow in your faith.

Some stories I have shared and will share in the next two books may seem amazing, yet all I have experienced so far is only a taste of what is possible through the gospel message. There are others who've operated in these truths to a much greater degree than I have. Yet Jesus is the perfect standard for how we can all walk —as heavenly people.

Conclusion

I pray that as you have read this, you have become more aware of God's goodness and that your faith has increased for what the Holy Spirit is able to accomplish in you. Jesus came to bring many sons to glory[148]— and you are one of them!

Now may God the Father give you a spirit of wisdom and revelation in the knowledge of himself. May the eyes of your heart be opened so that you know the hope to which he has called you, the riches of his glorious inheritance among the saints, and the immeasurable greatness of his power for us who believe.[149]

In Jesus' name, may you now be strengthened with power in your inner being through the Holy Spirit, according

---

[146] Ephesians 3:20
[147] Ephesians 4:13
[148] Hebrews 2:10
[149] Ephesians 1:17-19

the riches of God's glory, Christ the man of heaven dwelling in your heart through faith, rooted and grounded in love. May you come to understand and know by experience the love of God that surpasses knowledge, so that you may be filled with all the fullness of God.[150]

May the Holy Spirit do in and through your life, abundantly far more than all you can ask or imagine, by his power at work in you as you yield yourselves to him and grow in the knowledge of the Lord.[151] May you be filled with the knowledge of God's will in all spiritual wisdom and understanding, leading a life worthy of the Lord, bearing heavenly fruit in every good work, as you grow in the knowledge of the Lord.

May you be made strong with all the strength that comes from his glorious power, prepared to endure everything with patience, joy, and thanksgiving,[152] as you continually look into heaven and behold the glory of the Lord.

May the Lord of peace himself give you peace at all times in all ways,[153] so that the peace of God, which passes all understanding, will guard your heart and mind in Christ.[154] May the God of peace sanctify you entirely.[155] May the Lord make you increase and abound in love for everyone, strengthening your hearts in holiness,[156] so that when others see you they will see Jesus.

May the Lord Jesus himself, and God our Father, comfort your heart and strengthen you in every good work and word.[157] May the God of hope fill you with all joy and peace in believing, so that you will abound in hope by the power of the Holy Spirit.[158]

---

[150] Ephesians 3:16-19
[151] Ephesians 3:20
[152] Colossians 1:9-12
[153] 1Thessalonians 3:16
[154] Philippians 4:7
[155] 1 Thessalonians 5:23
[156] 1 Thessalonians 3:12-13
[157] 2 Thessalonians 2:16-17
[158] Romans 15:13

Chapter Nine—Heavenly Minded

May grace and peace be yours in abundance in the knowledge of God and of Jesus our Lord.[159] God who has called you is faithful, and he will do it![160]

---

[159] 2 Peter 1:2
[160] 1 Thessalonians 5:24

About The Author

Jonathan Brenneman was born in Rochester, New York and raised in Pennsylvania. Although a very troubled child he was at the same time very religious. He read the Bible from cover to cover when he was seven years old, all the while questioning and wondering about the existence of God.

When Jonathan was nine years old, he woke up one morning with bad back pain. His mother prayed for him, and to his surprise, he felt something like a hot ball of energy rolling up and down inside his back, and the pain melted away. It was shocking to say the least, but it convinced him God did exist! He later told his friends, *"I know that God is real. I felt his hand on my back."*

In spite of this experience, Jonathan still had no peace. He prayed the *"sinner's prayer"* but with no change until two years later when he had a *"born again"* experience. It felt like heaven opened and unexplainable joy and peace descended upon him! He was different, and knew it! The things he had felt so guilty about that he tried unsuccessfully to change, were simply gone.

After this time, Jonathan dedicated his life to the Lord as a missionary, going on his first mission trip at age fourteen. As a teenager and young adult he continued to travel and learn languages. Then, when he was twenty-one and during a time of desperation, Jonathan went to a Christian conference where he was very encouraged and touched by the Lord. It was a start of a supernatural lifestyle and growing in spiritual gifts during which time many amazing miracles and healings began to happen.

Jonathan worked in construction, but in between jobs he began to visit churches in the United States and Canada as well as in Latin America and Eastern Europe. His ministry journeys have included Russia, Ukraine, Poland, Italy, Canada, Mexico, Belize, and Brazil. In these places Jonathan has encouraged the believers and shared testimonies, and spoken with unbelievers and prayed for them. He also worked with children and seniors. He dedicated a lot of time to talking with, praying for, and encouraging people wherever he went, all the while growing in an experience of a love for people that is beyond understanding—for it is God's love. Jonathan believes it is a wonderful and tremendous privilege to be able to serve the people for whom Jesus gave his life.

Jonathan is now a missionary in Rio de Janeiro Brazil with his wife Elizabeth, and daughter Rebekah. He loves people, enjoys being with them, and rejoices at seeing what the Holy Spirit does in their lives. He likes to minister in the role of teaching, laying hands on the sick, visiting the elderly, and working with children—always loving them so they in turn will learn to love others with the love of God.

Contact

You can get in touch with Jonathan through his blog at www.gotoheavennow.com, at Goodreads, or through his Facebook author page, *Jonathan Brenneman*.

Amazon reviews are the author's tip jar! They also help to get the message out to more people. If you have enjoyed this book, please consider leaving a review on Goodreads and/or Amazon.com.

Also By Jonathan Brenneman

Of The "Heaven Now" Series
Part 2: I Will Awaken the Dawn

I Will Awaken the Dawn builds on the scriptural foundation laid in *Present Access to Heaven*. Learn from both scriptural insight and testimonies how to "Awaken the Dawn" of the knowledge of the glory of the Lord, with praise, thanksgiving, and declaration.

No matter how dark and impossible your surroundings may seem, they become heaven to you if your eyes are opened to see the Lord there. When you see that you are in heaven because you are in God's presence, heaven will begin to manifest around you. The earth is presently full of the glory of the Lord, but it will also be filled with the knowledge of the glory of the Lord, as the waters cover the seas!

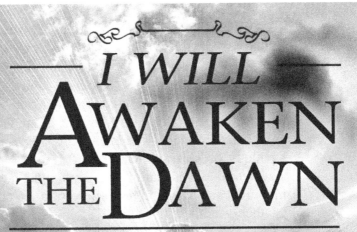

Part 3: Jesus Has Come In The Flesh

The Apostle John taught that every spirit confessing Jesus has come in the flesh is from God, and every spirit that does not confess Jesus is not from God, but is antichrist. (First John 4:2-3) *Jesus has Come in the Flesh* expounds on the implications of Jesus coming from heaven to live in an earthly human body. Understanding this truth can be used to test any spirit or teaching to see whether or not it is from God.

The influence of a spirit that denies Jesus has come in the flesh can be linked to every major problem in our societies, including sexual immorality, poverty, and violence. Learn to recognize the lies of the antichrist spirit which have infiltrated the church, and to root out the influence of the antichrist spirit from your thinking.

A spirit that denies Christ has come in the flesh opposes the tangible anointing of God's power and glory. Understanding the truth that Jesus has come in the flesh will cause you to walk in Holy Spirit anointing to bring about greater manifestations of God's power and glory in and through your life.

You will see how ministering physical healing demonstrates Jesus has come in the flesh; undoing the work of the devil and opposing the demonic onslaught of sexual immorality and violence in our societies. Read how the truths in *Jesus Has Come in the Flesh* have changed my life!

Other Books By Jonathan Brenneman

I Am Persuaded
Christian Leadership As Taught By Jesus

"Jonathan Brenneman in his *I Am Persuaded* provokes, jabs and challenges our sacred cows of church leadership. Yet, the jabs are not hurtful because they come from Scripture. This is not a reactionary book filled with leader bashing but a graceful and excellent presentation of mostly forgotten principles concerning how Jesus and the early church taught and practiced leadership.

All the key and at times controversial words are discussed: rule, obey, submission, apostles, authority, and spiritual covering. Excellent exegesis on these words is provided and is foundational to the author's conclusions. If you find yourself disagreeing, then, by all means, do a better exegesis. I think that will be difficult. Jonathan Brenneman has personally made a paradigm shift in his life and shares it with us. Will you?

I Am Persuaded is more than a fine Bible study, it is filled with real life stories which illustrate servant leadership. It is well written, fast paced, and provokes fresh thinking. I believe the reader and the church will be healthier when these principles are put into practice. Will you be persuaded? Will you undergo a paradigm shift? Read and find out. This is a good book and its message needs to be heard."

DR. STAN NEWTON—Missionary in Bulgaria;
Author: Glorious Kingdom.

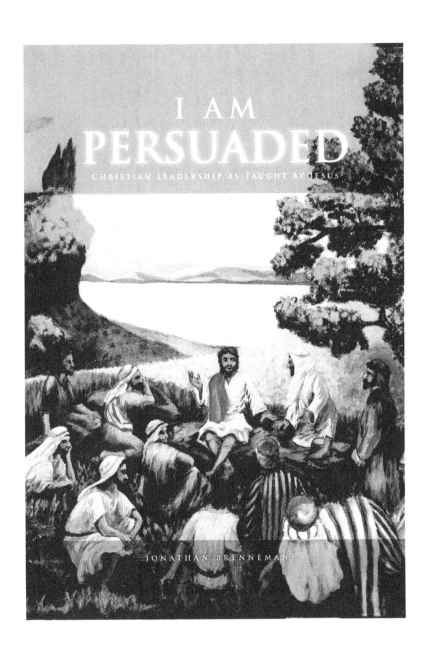

The Power-And-Love Sandwich

Why You Should Seek God's Face AND His Hand

If you've started to step out in the supernatural things of God, it's likely that you may have found yourself on the receiving end of a great deal of opposition. While you may have anticipated that those closest to you would be supportive and encouraging, instead your testimonies may have been met with a backlash. Fellow believers may have suggested that your focus on spiritual gifts is unbalanced. It may have been said that you're too preoccupied with signs and wonders.

In Jonathan Brenneman's book *The Power and Love Sandwich*, he explores the theological position of seeking God's face in conjunction with seeking His hand. Jonathan puts things into perspective and helps us to see through scripture that we don't have to pick one or the other. Both are liberally and unapologetically available to us. We can simultaneously embrace both the power of God and the love of God without having to forego one in order to embrace the other.

This book is a must read for those who intend to move in the power and love of God. You will learn to confidently walk in both the fruit of the Spirit as well as the gifts of the Spirit. The misguided objections of well-intended believers won't have the same power to break your spirit. Instead you will learn to shake it off, love them despite their opposition and remain kingdom focused.

CHERYL FRITZ—*Founder*
Inside Out Training and Equipping School

THE POWER & LOVE SANDWICH

Why You Should Seek Gods Face AND His Hand

Jonathan Breneman

Made in the USA
Monee, IL
12 October 2023